# *Philosophy of Mind*

## Mel Thompson

**TEACH YOURSELF BOOKS**

For UK order queries: please contact Bookpoint Ltd, 130 Milton Park, Abingdon, Oxon OX14 4SB. Telephone: (44) 01235 827720. Fax: (44) 01235 400454. Lines are open from 9.00–18.00, Monday to Saturday, with a 24-hour message answering service. Email address: orders@bookpoint.co.uk

For U.S.A. order queries: please contact McGraw-Hill Customer Services, P.O. Box 545, Blacklick, OH 43004-0545, U.S.A. Telephone: 1-800-722-4726. Fax: 1-614-755-5645.

For Canada order queries: please contact McGraw-Hill Ryerson Ltd., 300 Water St, Whitby, Ontario L1N 9B6, Canada. Telephone: 905 430 5000. Fax: 905 430 5020.

Long renowned as the authoritative source for self-guided learning – with more than 30 million copies sold worldwide – the *Teach Yourself* series includes over 300 titles in the fields of languages, crafts, hobbies, business and education.

*British Library Cataloguing in Publication Data*
A catalogue record for this title is available from The British Library.

*Library of Congress Catalog Card Number:* On file

First published in UK 2001 by Hodder Headline Plc, 338 Euston Road, London, NW1 3BH.

First published in US 2001 by Contemporary Books, A Division of The McGraw-Hill Companies, 1 Prudential Plaza, 130 East Randolph Street, Chicago, Illinois 60601 U.S.A.

The 'Teach Yourself' name and logo are registered trade marks of Hodder & Stoughton Ltd.

Copyright © 2001 Mel Thompson

Typeset by Transet Limited, Coventry, England.
Printed in Great Britain for Hodder & Stoughton Educational, a division of Hodder Headline Plc, 338 Euston Road, London NW1 3BH by Cox & Wyman Ltd, Reading, Berkshire.

Impression number    10 9 8 7 6 5 4 3 2
Year                        2007 2006 2005 2004 2003 2002

# CONTENTS

# INTRODUCTION

'Who am I?' is the most fundamental question that anyone can ask.

There are many superficial answers to it, but few are satisfactory. I have a name, but what does that mean? I can change my name without changing myself. I have friends and relatives, a career, a position in society; I am 'known' to a good number of people, who rely on me and predict how I will act. But if I live simply in order to fulfil their expectations is that authentic living? Am I no more than a product of what others expect? Could I go against everything that others have come to know about me and do something completely out of character and outrageous? Am I, even for a moment, really free to do whatever I like?

And does anyone else know the *real* me, anyway? They may guess what I am thinking, but they cannot actually know what goes on in my mind. Their idea of me is put together from what they have observed and what I have said. But that's hardly certain knowledge: I could be an actor, fooling them all. And if they do not know the real me, can I ever fully know anyone else? Am I alone in this world, except for what I can guess about other people?

When a relationship breaks down or a friend does something completely out of character, we may find it profoundly disturbing, because we rely on other people. We assume we know them and can trust them to act in a reasonably predictable way. We take for granted the fact that they have minds and personalities that they can be known, loved, feared or detested. But how – and to what extent – can we ever 'know' another person?

What is a 'person', anyway? Am I simply a complex body, controlled by patterns of electrical impulses in my brain? If so, do I change as my body changes? How can I possibly be the same 'person' from babyhood to old age? If alcohol, drugs, a severe blow to the head or a degenerative disease can change my personality, warping or destroying the 'mind' that has been known to other people, then am I really just a by-product of a physical body? Am I a zombie with an impotent 'mind' attached, fooling itself that it is in control of things, when all along it is controlled by the physical order?

And what does it mean to be conscious? Are animals conscious? They certainly appear to be, but does that give them a 'mind' like our own? And if so, should we be killing and eating them or trying to communicate with them?

What of computers? Is the brain sufficiently like a computer that, fed with a programme elaborate enough or the ability to learn for itself, a sufficiently powerful computer could actually become intelligent? Become a 'person' even? Perhaps machines have a primitive intelligence already? But, if so, what do we mean by intelligence?

# The structure of this book

Clearly, the philosophy of mind is an enormous field of study and a book such as this can do no more than touch on or outline some of the main debates and point to the questions that need to be addressed.

The first three chapters give a broad historical overview of the issues:

- From the earliest traditions of western philosophy, there has been discussion of the nature of the self and the mind. We shall look briefly at ideas about the self in Plato, Aristotle and later Greek thought, but also at the importance of the idea of the self or soul in later mediaeval thinking. 'Am I an eternal soul, trapped within the body? Do I have a destiny beyond this world?' Both in philosophical and religious terms, vital issues were raised during this period and many questions were framed, which are still discussed today.

- From the time of Descartes, in the 17th Century, the discussion of 'mind' became dominated by his dualistic idea of the mind as an unextended, thinking substance linked to a physical body. Discussions of Descartes and reactions against his thought, with a range of mind/body options spanning materialism, idealism and many different forms of dualism, were the core issue in the philosophy of mind right up to the second half of the 20th Century. During this time the debates were largely epistemological – concerned with the theory of knowledge. 'How can we know the mind? How can it affect and be affected by the physical world? Are mental attributes really no more than ways of describing or predicting bodily actions?'

■ From the mid-20th Century, however, the debates broadened and took into account the growth of computer science, artificial intelligence and the functional approach to the mind. There were also considerable advances in the understanding of the way in which the brain and nervous system works and so recent thinking in neurophysiology filtered through into the 'mind' debates. At the same time, linguistics developed as a separate discipline, raising a whole new range of issues about the function of communication. These disciplines together form a broad category of *cognitive science*. The key questions of this period are less 'Do we have an immortal soul?' or 'How can we prove the validity of ascribing a mental predicate?' and more 'What does the mind actually do? What difference does it make? How does it operate in processing sense experience and making decisions?'.

These three overview chapters are followed by a look at some of the traditional issues and problems in the philosophy of mind, relating them back to thinkers and approaches outlined in the first chapters:

■ How does the mind relate to the way we know things? Do we just passively receive data from the outside world or does the mind shape the world we experience?

- ■ What does it mean to be an individual? What gives me my identity?
- ■ Can I really know another person or am I just guessing from what I see and hear?
- ■ Am I free to act or is that simply an illusion in a totally determined physical world?
- ■ What is consciousness and can it be disembodied?

And in the final chapter, we shall be looking at creative aspects of the mind.

Warning! Be prepared for some nonsense! Some of the theories and conclusions in the philosophy of mind are what might politely be termed 'counter-intuitive' – in other words, they go against everything that common sense would expect. To say that the physical world is actually no more than a feature of our mind or that a headache is no more than a disposition to hold one's head, look glum and reach for aspirin, is clearly nonsense.

Take it from me, the physical world does exist and headaches are real enough even if you give no visible indication of your suffering. Philosophers have the infuriating habit of driving arguments to their logical conclusion, even if they appear to have left the realm of sanity in order to do so. Sometimes the important thing is to follow the logic of the argument, even if the conclusion appears to be less than sensible.

But above all, remember that you have the ultimate criterion for assessing all such theories: you have a mind. You are using it at this moment. As your eyes are scanning these lines, neurones are firing in your brain and energy is being used. Whatever your mind is, it is engaged in interpreting these marks on paper, forming concepts and relating them to a whole network of meanings that you have learned. The ideas themselves are being assessed and related to all that you have experienced in your life so far. And all of this is happening automatically, in what has become a normal mental function – reading. Perhaps, the final question to ask of all theories is this: *Does this make sense of what I experience myself to be?*

# 1 | FROM THE GREEKS TO THE SIXTEENTH CENTURY

The Greek word that most obviously describes the self or mind is *psyche*, from which of course, we get the word psychology. But the psyche was not exactly what we would call mind, since it was often used in a much wider sense as the power of a living thing to grow and move and have an effect upon its surroundings, as well as to will something to happen and the other aspects of what we would call 'mental states'. Thus, for example, both Plato and Aristotle thought that plants had psyche, and the very first philosopher and scientist, Thales of Miletus (6th Century BCE), described magnets as having psyche because of their power to move other things and declared that 'all things are full of gods', implying that psyche is universal.

Notice, therefore, that the ancient philosophers looked at mental states, without trying to relate them to a separate, immaterial substance called 'mind'. The psyche was much broader; it was the power of a being to grow and change and act. In other words, you do not have to have a separate, invisible thing called a 'mind' in order to do those things, psyche was simply the word used to describe those aspects of a living thing.

The ancients were as much scientists as philosophers, concerned to produce theories of explanation. Democritus (b. mid-5th Century BCE), who analysed everything in terms of atoms in space, thought that the psyche comprised the very simplest of atoms (spherical ones); Heraclitus (540–480 BCE), concerned always with the process of change, thought that the psyche was a kind of transforming fire. The Pythagoreans (as described by Plato in *Timaeus*) thought of the psyche as a controlling and balancing principle of harmony for the body.

The ancients were also influenced by the idea of reincarnation. Herodotus knew of the Egyptian idea of an immortal soul being able to leave a body at death and move into another about to be born. Indeed, Pythagoras (*c.* 570–497 BCE), who was a notable philosopher as well as a mathematician, held that the souls of those who had died could enter into animals for their future lives.

---

**COMMENT**

The implications of reincarnation for Greek thought are quite profound. If there is a soul (or psyche) that can enter into an animal after having been a human, then it cannot be identified *exclusively* with the thinking element of the self – otherwise you would end up with 'thinking' animals. Rather a psyche that is able to be reincarnated is much broader, comprising the basic power to animate a body and give it character.

In the next chapter, when we come to Descartes, we shall consider his dualism of an unextended, thinking mind and an extended physical body. The psyche of the ancient Greeks was far more than that and for the mind in the narrower sense of a thinking element, the Greeks would have used the term *nous*.

A key question in the philosophy of mind is therefore whether one should be considering 'mind' (in the narrow sense of a thinking self) at all or rather the broader concept of psyche. The philosophy of mind is sometimes called philosophical psychology, but it should be clear that – at least in Cartesian terms – the two disciplines are not identical. Psychology deals with the thinking, feeling, perceiving, acting self – it is a self that does far more than just think about itself in order to know that it exists!

---

## An immortal soul?

A good starting point for examining Plato's view of the soul lies with the source of his original inspiration – Socrates. Plato (427–347 BCE) presents Socrates (469–399 BCE) as a thinker who was concerned above all with the question about what it means to live well. In other words, he is concerned with the nature and purpose of a human life – that which raises the human above the animal. When Socrates was condemned, he accepted death calmly, not thinking of himself as limited to his physical body. For Socrates, the self is largely non-physical and the body is not the true person. His task, shown in his challenge to conventional thought and in his acceptance of death, was to explore the spiritual, or non-material aspects of human life.

Plato has a dualism of immaterial substance (psyche) and physical body. He believes that the psyche is immortal and gives two reasons for that:

1 In *Timaeus*, he argues that it is an essential feature of the psyche to be self-moving, since it is the power to move and change other things, rather than being itself moved by the physical body. Without a psyche, we have only a corpse – therefore, the psyche must have pre-dated the body it inhabits.

2 He argues that the psyche has knowledge of the 'forms' rather than simply of the particulars (see the discussion of the forms in *TY Philosophy*, p. 27f), but since the forms are immaterial and eternal, so also is the psyche, since – in order to understand the world of the forms – it must in some way share their world.

Later, in Phaedo, Plato was to change his theory somewhat. Instead of seeing the psyche as responsible for animating and giving rise to human activity and mental states, he limits the mind to the reasoning part and leaves emotions and other aspects of human life – like the ability to perceive and respond to something – to the realm of the body.

By the time he wrote *The Republic*, however, he saw the psyche as more complex and allowed that it was concerned with all aspects – both those connected with emotion and activity and those connected with thought.

In *The Republic*, he makes the analogy between the city and the soul. Just as the soul has three parts – reason, the spirited (or seat of passions) and the basic appetites – so the city has its philosopher-rulers or guardians, those who defend it and make it work, and the workers, who seek only the satisfaction of their needs. The self, therefore, for Plato includes, but is not limited to, the reasoning part. The ideal life is one in which all three aspects of the self are balanced. The basic appetites are held in check by the active faculties, which are themselves guided by reason. The good life is achieved through integrity, not elimination. He does not deny the appetites and actions, but places them firmly under the control of reason.

---

**COMMENT**

Overall, there is a sense that, for Plato, the self has as its goal an understanding of the good and the beautiful and that it is capable of doing this in spite of the hazards, frustrations and limitations of the particular things with which we are surrounded in this life. The impulse – led by reason, but not limited to reason – is to aspire to something higher. Thus, given the choice of seeking truth or pleasure, Plato suggests that we should opt for truth, since pleasure is limited and transient. The mind is that which aspires to higher things, an important feature of his thinking that has implications for religion and the arts, as well as for philosophy.

---

Plato has been enormously influential in this area, partly because – through the neo-Platonists and then Christian philosophers like St Augustine – his views have been introduced into the Christian world-view, which formed the background of so much western thought. Partly also because, unlike the pre-Socratics who speculated about the nature of mind, Plato relates the mind to broader issues of psychology – to the questions of ethics, knowledge and the appreciation of beauty, and to the basic question of what it means to lead the good life. In other words, Plato sets the agenda: he shows that questions about the self are fundamental to the issue of how we can know things, how we should relate to one another and how we should seek personal balance and integrity.

**Entombed**

For Plato, there is a real feeling that the self has come down to Earth from its natural heavenly abode and is entombed within the physical body, but at the same time – through reason and knowledge of the forms – it cannot help but betray its origins. This is emphasised by the pun that arises in the Greek, for the body (*soma*) becomes the tomb (*sema*) of the soul. Its goal is to escape upwards.

However, Plato's concern for the distinction between soul and body should not lead us to assume that he saw individuals as in some way arriving on earth fully formed. He took the view (e.g. in *The Republic*, Book 6) that people were like plants, developing according to the soil in which they are planted, arguing that the soul takes on the characteristics of its environment. He was also very aware of the ability of society to influence the individual. Clearly, Plato wants to account for the very obvious influence that nurture and environment have on individuals, but at the same time, he sees the thinking part as pre-dating the body and being linked with the eternal realm of forms.

**COMMENT**

This raises a broad but fascinating issue, which is seen most keenly in the case of the very gifted. Is the genius, the brilliant musician, artist, writer or philosopher 'born' as such or is he or she simply the product of heredity and environment? Is there anything in their background that can 'explain' a Shakespeare or a Mozart?

For Plato and his three aspects of the self, the thinking element is primary and has responsibility for guiding the others. Logically, therefore, philosophers should strive to remain philosophers, even if the environment within which they find themselves is not conducive to their craft. Emotions and basic urges may have shaped Mozart's day-to-day living, but in any overall assessment, the primary element is that which links him with the realm of the eternal.

## Making us what we are

The shorthand way of describing Aristotle's view of the soul and its relationship to the body is to say that the soul of an axe is cutting, the soul of an eye is seeing and the soul of a man is thinking. In other words, everything has a form or an essence, which is shown in its primary activity. *The soul is what makes a thing what it is.*

Aristotle (384-322 BCE) thought that all living things had souls and that the psyche was a 'principle of life' – that which distinguishes the living from the inanimate. Within the range of creatures having souls, there was a subset, namely those who were also capable of rational thought. Thus the rational 'mind' is part of but not identical with the psyche.

**Note**

The Greek term for the thinking mind is nous as opposed to the more general term psyche. As we shall see throughout this book, it is debatable whether one should consider the rational mind in isolation from the broader questions of psychology. For the Greeks, however, nous held a special place as intellect, the highest and most distinctive of human functions.

Aristotle rejected Plato's idea of the psyche as an immaterial substance, but also rejected the atomists view of it as a fine and extended physical thing and the Pythagorean approach of seeing it as the agent of balance within the body.

In *On the Soul* (Book 2), Aristotle makes the point that a body can be divided into its component parts, but those are parts of its matter, not parts of its 'form' or 'essence'. Now this suggests that, when we are dealing with the mind, we should not assume that it might in some way be shown as existing in among the various parts into which the body can be divided. Just because it cannot be found located in parts of the brain or other physical system, does not make it any less part of the 'essence' of a person.

Aristotle sees the psyche as the form that organises the material body into what it essentially is. Notice that this makes the psyche distinct from the material body, but not separate from it. You do not have the body in one place and the soul somewhere else – they are locked together, the former given its shape and characteristics by the latter. The soul is thus the actuality of the body as an organised thing. Aristotle is therefore able to dismiss the question whether the soul and the body are one. Using his own analogy, it is as meaningless to ask this as to ask whether the wax and the shape given to it by the stamp are one. You cannot separate matter from that of which it is the matter.

---

**COMMENT**

A statue remains a piece of marble. You cannot separate out the marble from the statue. You cannot point to that which is statue but not marble; and to think that 'statue' must refer to something other than that which the marble forms is nonsense. However, as we shall see later, such nonsense was still being railed against by Gilbert Ryle in the 20th Century, in what he termed a 'category mistake', even though Aristotle had dealt with it quite adequately more than two millennia earlier. Sadly, however, Ryle concluded that 'statue' was simply a way of describing marble, which is also nonsense.

---

Aristotle then goes on to give his definition of a soul as a thing's essence.

And this is clarified by an example:

> Suppose that the eye were an animal – sight would have been its soul, for sight is the substance, or essence, of the eye... the eye being merely the matter of seeing; when seeing is removed the eye is no longer an eye, except in name.

> As the pupil *plus* the power of sight constitutes the eye, so the soul *plus* the body constitutes the animal.

> From this it indubitably follows that the soul is inseparable from its body, or at any rate that certain parts of it are (if it has parts) – for the actuality of some of them is nothing but the actualities of their bodily parts.

**COMMENT**

From time to time, as you read through the arguments presented in this book, refer back to this quotation from Aristotle. I have a feeling that much time and effort in the philosophy of mind could have been saved had his principles been attended to more carefully. We shall see later that what he has to say – namely that the soul or mind is distinct from particular material parts of the body, that it is holistic and that it is inseparable from the body – has implications for much modern discussion about materialism and functionalism and also the approach of philosophers like John Searle, in distinguishing the many different layers of life and the concepts appropriate to each. What Aristotle is surely saying here is that the way you describe a soul or the essence of an animal – human or otherwise – depends on, but is not reducible to, what one might say about parts of that animal body, including (most importantly) its brain.

Thus we find that, for Aristotle, the self or mind is the essence or form of a human being, an essence that is distinct from but also inseparable from the material body.

Naturally, however, there then needs to be a distinction between the 'soul' in the sense of being an independent, living thing (as seen in animals) and being a distinctively 'thinking' animal, as in humankind. This distinction is important because much modern debate concerns consciousness, along with sensations, emotions, responses and the like. These are features of life that humans share with animals. By the same token, the principle form of dualism, stemming from Descartes and against which so much subsequent debate has been pitched, is a dualism of extended body and thinking mind — with thought as the sole function and criterion that separates mind and body.

## Form and change

It is worth taking Aristotle's argument into account when considering the process of change and personal identity. When particular material parts of oneself change – whether through amputation or ageing – there remains an overall form that realises the capacities of the body and gives it an overall coherence. That is the soul, or substance, or form; it gives motion and life. It is what is distinctive about each living thing. To change the form of something it would be necessary to change the whole meaning and essence of the thing – form is not located, but is a principle of definition and of recognition. As we said earlier, it is what makes a thing what it is.

### Example

Suppose you fall into the hands of a skilled transplant surgeon. He (or she) can remove parts of your body and replace them by others. You gradually find yourself composed of material that was not part of the original you. But you still have an identity. Your 'form' is the overall shape given to that material (and not physical shape – but sense of identity) and this cannot be considered on the same level as the bits and pieces that are removed and replaced. Form is holistic; it is what the whole of you is, no matter which bits of you may be expressing it at any particular time. It is something you have before the surgery began and which does not depend upon the various parts of which you are composed.

In Mary Shelley's *Frankenstein*, there is a dramatic moment when the creature that Frankenstein has constructed from various human 'materials' comes to life. Soon this monstrous replica of a human being starts to develop thought and emotion, responding in horror to the enormity of its artificial birth with terrible results.

*Frankenstein* exposes the hubris of science, assuming that it can analyse and then reassemble the human person, without paying a terrible price for venturing into an area in which mechanical analysis and assembly simply will not suffice. Any human subject viewed merely as a construction of parts becomes a monster.

## Body and soul

If the soul is what gives the body its form, bringing it forth as a living individual, then we need to recognise just how close the relationship between body and soul becomes. We do not have a body, with its own form and performing its own actions, to which a secondary, invisible thing called a 'soul' is added. The term 'soul' describes that which shapes and gives life to the body.

Consider the analogy of the actor on stage. The performer transforms himself into the character being portrayed. That character is displayed in terms of words, actions, gestures and responses. The illusion is created that the performer is lost within the part. The Aristotelian approach is to see the soul as the character being displayed, not as some hidden actor behind that character. This contrasts with the Platonic approach, where the eternal soul is more like the actor, with an eternal and therefore ongoing life quite apart from this particular incarnation.

## Later Greek thought

Later, philosophers were to revert to more materialist ways of thinking about the self. Epicurus (341–271 BCE), like Democritus earlier, took an atomist view of reality. That is, he thought that the whole of reality could be seen as made up of physical bodies (atoms) in a void. The soul or self could not be void; therefore he needed to find some way of describing it in physical terms. He saw it as atoms, spread throughout the body, animating it – rather like a wind passing through and around a physical structure. The problem was always how this kind of physical reality could be related to the process of thought and perception.

Epicurus and others objected to the Platonic notion of an immortal and immaterial substance on the grounds (among others) that such a psyche could neither act nor be acted on, since it would have no direct link with the physical and mutable world.

**Note**
Notice here a fundamental feature of the mind/body problem. If the mind is physical, it is difficult to see how it can originate the process of thought and choice, being caught up in the web of physical causality. Contrariwise, if it is *not* physical, it is difficult to see how it can exert an influence on the physical world. In other words – putting it crudely – *either it can't decide what to do or it can't do it.*

The Stoics considered the soul to be like breath (*pneuma*), permeating and animating the body, giving it the ability to move about and relate to the world. They also introduced an important concept – that of representations (*phantasia*). When we perceive something, an idea of that thing is formed in the mind – a 'representation' of the object. We cannot know anything except by way of these representations. We must also have a perception of ourselves before we can start to be aware of our world. Even animals, by showing fear in the face of something stronger than themselves or aggression in the face of an attacker must have some awareness of what they are and of their relative place in the scheme of things. Without such basic awareness, their responses to the external world would make no sense.

The Stoics went one step further, claiming that whatever was known through representations, could also be described. Every representation has its *lekton* or ability to be articulated. In other words, the mind plays an important role in receiving and naming experiences. But such reception is only half the story. The mind then gives assent to what it perceives. In other words, it makes value judgements, either approving or disapproving, and then acting accordingly.

According to Epictetus (50–120), our personal identity comes from our moral character, which consists in making good use of the representations we receive. The self is not simply our reasoning faculty, but the application of our reason in selecting our goals and shaping our course in life.

For the Stoics, there is a fundamental difference between a human being and an animal. Animals simply respond automatically to the stimuli they are given. A human being is able to reflect on the stimuli, to appreciate them and to choose how to respond to them. The whole of moral and social life follows from this.

Our consciousness is the collection of all the *phantasia* that we receive and our selfhood is seen in the way in which we understand and respond to those *phantasia*. In a sense, the interest has shifted from physical considerations of how a non-extended thing such as a soul can encounter the world, to seeing what it does about it. We may not be able to show that our experience matches reality, but we at least know that we have an experience. *We display selfhood by dealing with those experiences.*

Part of that is rational, but the self is more than reason. It is the overall agent in shaping our lives. This means that there need be no separate rational part. Rather, the whole of the self's controlling power (its *hegemonikon*), located in the heart, was responsible for this process of receiving and responding to impressions from outside. Thus, the Stoics appear to allow a physical basis for the self, at least in the sense that it made no sense to speak of a self that was separable from the physical body through which it acted.

Against the Stoics, Plotinus (205–270) and other neo-Platonists continued the tradition of the separate soul and body, although they generally held that the brain was the seat of the perceptions. They held that the self was both aware and self-aware at the same time and that the whole of the self was present in every part of the body. In other words, unlike the Stoics, they were concerned to remove any possibility of physical location. The soul was real, but not physical.

Plotinus discusses the soul particularly in Book 4 of his *Enneads*. The soul was distinct from the body, because the body itself was composite and needed to be ordered, directed and given life by the soul. Without the soul, the body is dissolved.

Notice here that there is a restatement of the Platonic dualism of soul and body, but taking into account some elements of Aristotle's view of the soul as giving form and order. This reflects the general position of the neo-Platonists, who would not have thought of themselves as having that label, but were simply restating Plato in the light of subsequent criticism.

As with the later mediaeval thinkers, there is also an important religious and moral element. Thus, life in the body is essentially evil and limited, whereas the soul can look forward to its own good through the exercise of virtue and can look to a non-physical destiny. In all ways the soul is superior to the bodily state, although in this life it is expressed through the body, which it fills and directs.

Plotinus also saw the soul as descending into matter, passing through the various heavenly realms as it did so and therefore he was able to argue that the patterns of the heavenly bodies could influence our earthly life, since at one time, before our appearance on earth, we had a celestial body. Thus, the soul arrives on earth with its character and dispositions already formed and after this life it is destined to ascend again to the higher realm.

---

**IN OTHER WORDS**

- For the neo-Platonists, as for Plato, the soul was essentially immortal and separable from the body.
- For the Epicureans, it was a fine physical substance.
- For Aristotle; it was the form of the body.
- For the Stoics, the soul was that which was self aware, and also which encountered and understood the world through 'representations' and therefore language, issuing in the ability to evaluate and act morally. To use the modern term, the stoics saw the self in terms of 'consciousness'.

---

It is commonly pointed out that most issues in western philosophy can be traced back to Ancient Greece and the philosophy of mind is no exception. The atomists and epicureans took a view that has echoes in modern materialism and behaviourism, and even aspects of neuroscience and artificial intelligence — since they saw the mental aspects of life as embodied. By contrast, the Platonic approach separating mind and body, leads to modern dualism. The Aristotelian and Stoic views have mind and body as distinct, but much more closely linked, with the Stoics anticipating much modern thought in terms of distinctive human self-expression and language.

As we shall see in the next chapter, many of the issues from the time of Descartes into the 20th Century arose from the desire to make a clear distinction between mind and body and yet recognise the degree to which mind interacts with the physical world. The arguments may have changed, but the issues were very familiar to the Ancient Greeks.

# The soul and its fate

In assessing mediaeval views of the soul or self, it is important to recognise that, prior to the 13th Century when Aristotle's works were translated and studied in European universities, there was a lack of secular philosophy, in the sense of a discussion of key issues without reference to an overall religious view of life, based on Christian teachings. Even with the coming of Aristotelianism, thinkers like Aquinas saw it as their task to reconcile such philosophy with Christian teaching. Hence the title of this section is 'the soul and its fate', because that was the issue of concern to religious thinkers during that period.

Of ancient philosophy, the tradition that most directly influenced the developing thought of Christendom was that of Plato – although there were also influences from the Stoics. This is seen particularly in writings of St Augustine (354–430), who contrasted the changing and fallen nature of the physical world with the unchanging, eternal realm of ideas. He saw the soul as a special substance whose task was to rule the body. It was endowed by God with reason and could only be known through reason. Of course, he also believed that through the 'Fall' humankind was not as God had intended it to be and that its intellect was dimmed and its will weakened.

Nevertheless, in contrast to the material body, the mind was able to rise above the changing world and have true knowledge of immutable ideas. The mind could be known through introspection. In a curious anticipation of the famous argument of Descartes ('I think, therefore I am') Augustine held that the existence of the mind was certain, for even if (following the sceptics) I could believe that I was deceived about most things, nevertheless I must exist in order to be deceived. *I cannot therefore be deceived about my own existence.*

He also took the view, which is interesting in terms of the part the mind plays in the theory of knowledge, that the senses themselves could not provide us with knowledge. True, they provided the sensations that were the basis of knowledge, but true knowledge required the exercise of reason to interpret those sensations.

Thus, for Augustine, the mind is a divine gift, ruling the body, linking with the eternal world of ideas, knowable only by reflection. This provides a very clear dualism of body and mind, which was to influence Descartes and, through him, much of the modern debate about the philosophy of mind.

The self or soul was thus seen as fallen, inhabiting a physical body, but essentially connected with the higher world. At death, body and soul separate, the body to return to corruption, the soul to go to judgement and either heaven or hell. For religious reasons, therefore, it was crucial that body and soul were separable. Any theory which made the soul a by-product of bodily processes (the 'epiphenomenon' of later debates) would fail to take into account either it's being a divine endowment, or its being able to have an eternal destiny once its temporal body was no more.

---

**COMMENT**

Many of the debates in the philosophy of mind have taken place against a background of religious (particularly Christian) thought. Materialism and behaviourism seem to go hand in hand with a secular focus and a sense that language about God makes him as elusive or meaningless as a separate 'self'. Equally, those who have defended some form of dualism and thus of the theoretical separation of mind and body, may have been influenced by this approach in the religious thinking of the west.

---

# 2 DUALISM AND ITS ALTERNATIVES

The philosophy of mind includes the exploration of a whole range of possible relationships between mind and body and some thinkers want to eliminate either one or the other. On the one side, there is the idea that the only real thing is the physical world of bodies, examinable by science (*materialism* and *behaviourism*); on the other is the less common view that all we can know are the phenomena we experience in our minds and that it is the physical world that is uncertain or only known through or put together by the mind (*idealism*).

Most philosophers, however, have come to the view that both minds and bodies are real and that they are somehow related to one another (*dualism*). How exactly they are related is a further problem and so we have a whole variety of forms of dualism, reflecting different ideas about that relationship.

## Dualism

Although we have already come across dualism in Plato and in Augustine, in terms of the modern debate about minds and bodies, the most significant thinker was Descartes (1596–1650). Many of the theories about how minds and bodies affect one another have developed in order to answer questions raised by Descartes' theory.

### 'I think therefore I am'

At a time when scepticism was rife, Descartes was concerned to find some point of certainty from which he could start to build up a structure of genuine knowledge. He was aware that his senses could sometimes deceive him and therefore resolved never to trust them. He supposed that some malign force was able to make him doubt all that he generally accepted as true. Was there anything that he could not doubt?

His conclusion – one of the most famous in the history of philosophy – was that he could not doubt himself as a thinking being, for the very act of doubting required thought: *cogito ergo sum*, 'I think, therefore I am'.

---

**COMMENT**

Descartes may indeed have reached the conclusion *cogito ergo sum* from first principles, but he was not the first to do so. St Augustine had come to the same conclusion in *De Trinitate*, Book X, his version being *si fallor, sum* – in order for one to be deceived and in error, one must exist.

---

But what was this self that Descartes could not doubt? 'I think, therefore I am' implied a radical distinction between the world of matter, known to the senses, and the mental world, known (at least in one's own case) directly.

He therefore concluded that mind and matter were utterly different things. Matter was extended in space; mind was unextended. Matter was known to the senses; mind was not. This radical dualism immediately caused problems. First, the 'self' was now reduced to just one aspect of being a person – thought. Humans were mechanical bodies, with unextended minds attached. How then could you ever know anybody else's mind? You could not encounter it through the senses, for it was not part of the physical world. How might your own mind actually make a difference in the physical world?

Before examining dualism any further, one needs to guard against seeing the mind as some kind of subtle, invisible body, existing in the world of space and time, yet not subject to its usual rules of cause and effect. This is a rather crude caricature of what Descartes and other dualists have actually claimed, but it is a caricature that has often been taken for reality and it was presented by Gilbert Ryle in *The Concept of Mind* (1949), a most influential book for an understanding of the mind/body issue, where he called Cartesian dualism the 'official view' and labelled the mind 'the Ghost in the Machine'. We shall look at this particular criticism a little later (page 37)

The essential thing to realise is that, for Descartes, mental reality is not a part of the empirical world and therefore not in the world of space. The mind is not to be found in the brain, or any other part of the body. It may be related to the body, but is certainly not some occult set of physical causes and effects. That is why the 'Ghost in the Machine' is no more than a caricature.

Descartes considered that mind was an immaterial substance, distinct from the physical substance of the body. Mental states were therefore related to this invisible thing. This 'substantial' way of approaching mind has long since gone out of fashion, even among dualists.

As we shall see later, a major criticism of the whole Cartesian way of considering minds and bodies was set out by Gilbert Ryle in *The Concept of Mind*. Whether or not one can accept his positive proposals for giving meaning to language about minds, his negative task of demolishing Descartes' 'Ghost in the Machine' is quite devastating. He pointed out that Descartes, accepting that the physical world could be seen in terms of mechanics, tried to define the mind negatively, as that which was non-physical, non-extended and so on. As a result of this, he suggests that Descartes saw the mind as in some way as analogous to a body, but without the physical nature, in other words, as a non-physical machine.

## The pineal gland

The problem Descartes faced was that he had a mechanical view of the physical world – and indeed, his mechanics depended upon the contact between bodies, without any of the benefit of Newton's idea of 'forces'. He therefore needed to show that there was some physical point in the body through which the non-physical, non-extended mind could actually operate to effect changes in the physical world.

In other words, he accepted that an absolute separation of mind and body could not be possible, for otherwise the mind could make absolutely no difference. Without some point of interaction there was no way of explaining how mental actions (e.g. feeling something or wanting something) can have physical results (e.g. flinching in response to pain or reaching out to take the desired object).

Descartes believed that the point of contact was the pineal gland, located between the left and right sides of the brain. He considered – thinking in terms of contact mechanics – that the very slightest movement in this gland would have a great affect on the course of the 'animal spirits'.

How an unextended mind can cause even the slightest movement in a physical body, remained a theoretical problem – but Descartes tucked that problem away in the most inaccessible place possible, but in a place, between the halves of the brain, where it seemed most likely that the mind would make its difference.

## My mind?

A key worry about Descartes' form of dualism is that one can refer to 'my mind'. But if 'my mind' means anything at all, then it implies that there is a sense of self that *transcends* the mind. If I were nothing but thought, then the conclusion to Descartes famous process of systematic doubt should not have been 'I think therefore I am' but simply 'There is thought'. The mere fact that thought is the one thing that cannot be doubted should not be taken to imply that a human being is *no more than* a thinking thing attached to a mechanical body. Few would challenge the idea that the process of thinking is a major part of what it is to be human; but is it all we mean by the self? Clearly, if 'my mind' has any significance, then it is not.

The real problem with Descartes' legacy on this issue is that generations of philosophers have struggled with the idea of mechanical bodies somehow taking on purposeful action, and wondering how on earth a non-physical, non-extended mind could bring that about.

**Interactionism**

Dualism claims that mind and the body are distinct, but act upon one another. If you break a leg (a bodily phenomenon) you will experience pain (a mental phenomenon). If you get excited or afraid (or both at once!), your body reacts accordingly.

Interactionism is a general term for theories that seek to relate the mental and physical realms to one another. There are many varieties of interactionism, some of which we shall outline here.

## Occasionalism

Occasionalism is a theory, associated particularly with the Cartesian thinker Malebranche (1638–1715), which takes Descartes' dualism to its logical conclusion. If mind and body are completely separate, there seems no way that the one can have a direct causal effect on the other – there is no mechanism for getting across what was to become known as 'Leibniz' gap' (see opposite). How then could mental events and physical events fit so closely together that they give the impression of being causally linked? How is it that, at the moment I feel pleased to see someone, my mouth stretches out in a smile?

Malebranche's answer to this is that, at the same moment that I feel happy, my face smiles. The two things happen separately but on the same occasion and they are kept synchronised by God. I feel happy; God stretches my mouth.

**COMMENT**

This has always seemed to me to be a most implausible theory, quite apart from any issues of religious belief. If there is no mechanism that will allow my mind to influence the physical world, how does God do so? Presumably God is not thought of as a physical being – so what enables his 'mind' to establish a mechanism to do what mine cannot?

## Pre-established harmony

Still on the religious theme, we come to Leibniz (1646–1716), whose concept of pre-established harmony goes beyond Malebranche, in that God does not have to intervene constantly to ensure that my body does what my mind would like to do but cannot. For Leibniz, therefore, there is a harmony between mind and matter that is established by God, so that, although the mind appears to be directing what happens to the physical body, in actual fact the physical body is running within an enclosed physical system that only happens to coincide with the mental one. Between the two there remains the 'gap' (hence the term 'Leibniz' gap' for the disjunction of mind and body).

The mind does not actually make any difference to the physical world, in the sense of being a cause of physical movement, but only appears to do so, because of the coincidence of the two systems.

This theory is closely linked to Leibniz' view of physical reality. He held that everything is divisible again and again until you arrive at the simplest possible entities. But these would not have physical extension (for, if they did, they could be divided further) and if they are not physical, they must be mental – since, following Descartes – everything is either physical and extended, or mental and unextended. Leibniz called these entities *monads*. Every complex being therefore comprises countless monads. How do they all work together to produce intelligent activity? Leibniz argued that there must be a pre-established harmony, without which organisation would be quite impossible.

---

**COMMENT**

Clearly, Leibniz has a good religious reason for taking this view. It enabled him to introduce the idea of purpose back into a universe that could otherwise be seen as an impersonal mechanism. Purpose and co-operation between mechanical entities was established by God. It is only natural, therefore, that the harmony between mental choice and physical action should follow from this same ordering of nature.

## Epiphenomenalism

From an evolutionary perspective, it is clear that the more advanced and complex a creature, the more likely it is for it to have what we would recognise as a mind or consciousness. Comparing something as complex as the brain and nervous system of a human being with that of some primitive creature or with an inanimate object it seems clear that, in some way, the mind is a product of the complexity of physical systems.

This approach leads to the view that mind is the natural by-product of an increasingly complex brain and nervous system. The various things that I think about, imagine, or picture in my mind are therefore *epiphenomena*. They arise out of (and are caused by) the electrical impulses that move between brain cells, but they are not actually part of those physical phenomenon – they are 'above' (*epi-*) those phenomena.

Now there is one obvious but crucial problem with this approach, namely that the mind becomes impotent. If it is produced by the physical system, rather than being able to interact with it, it cannot make a difference. Consciousness does not modify behaviour, for behaviour is part of the physical world, influenced only by physical causes – at most, consciousness may give us the illusion of control.

### Example

The smell of cooking may tell you what is in the oven. But the smell does not influence the process of cooking – however much it may serve as a guide to what is going on. So if mental phenomena are given off by brain activity, they may show you what is happening, but cannot themselves make anything happen.

The key feature here is that epiphenomenalism allows the physical world to retain its closed system of causality. Yet the mind is produced by the brain – hence the amazing way in which we think that our mind has influenced our body. It only appears to do so; in fact it is simply the product of the physical system.

**IN OTHER WORDS**

My arm needs to be raised and my brain puts this into effect, but at the same time, there is the additional effect of a 'mental' product of my deciding to raise my arm. But that mental product has not pre-dated the process that will lead to the arm being raised.

**COMMENT**

This has always struck me as one of the daftest of the many daft theories in the philosophy of mind. It goes counter to experience, where the decision to act, or even the process of worrying about whether or not to act, comes before the action itself. As you watch a cat about to pounce on a mouse or a child waiting for exactly the moment to press a button in a computer game, there is a complex set of relationships between observational inputs and the anticipation of a physical output. The process of holding one's breath and waiting for exactly the right moment is one that requires mental effort and is a sign of the sophistication of sentient beings. To see mental activity simply as a by-product of a set of physical causes seems highly improbable. It only makes sense if we are thinking of 'mind' in the crudest form of substance dualism. The complexity of the operation that, on a physical level, the brain carries out is what we both describe  and experience as the working of a conscious mind.

It is difficult to see how an epiphenomenalist position could really explain the process of writing a novel, for example. If the mind is simply a by-product of physical brain activity, with no way of influencing physical action, then the novel is not something 'thought up' at all. It is not the product of creative thought, but the inevitable result of a set of physical causes. Shakespeare's mind had no part in writing his plays, they were simply the product of a process generated by electrical impulses in his brain – his mind, his thoughts as the plays were being written, his insights, were no more than a by-product of a complex neural process. I find that quite unconvincing.

**COMMENT**

How, on this theory, could anyone distinguish between a creative activity and a purely mechanical one? How do I know you are an intelligent individual rather than a robot, if whatever mind you have cannot have any effect on your speech or actions? In the end, epiphenomenalism seems little more than materialism with a private picture show attached!

## Double Aspect theory

Spinoza (1632–1677) took the view that God and nature were one and the same and that all reality has both a mental and a physical aspect to it. Rather than having two very different substances, physical and mental, Spinoza argued that there was a single substance that was both conscious and extended. The mind and body could not be separated, and were, in effect, two ways of seeing the same thing. Every event that we experience as mental must therefore also have a physical aspect.

This view, sometimes called the 'identity hypothesis', effectively argues that neural events and conscious experiences are simply two ways of explaining the same thing. In other words, thinking is the inner aspect of which the outer or scientifically examinable aspect is brain activity.

In terms of a description of what is going on when an intelligent action is being performed, one could say that human beings have properties that are non-physical, but that such properties do not imply that there is a separate, non-physical 'substance' called mind. This is sometimes referred to as the 'property theory' of mind and it is maintained by those who want to retain a definite dualism, but try to avoid the problems of arguing for a mental substance of some sort. A single substance can have both types of property – mental and physical – applied to it.

## Property dualism

The dualism of Descartes, as we have seen is one that distinguished between two forms of substance, physical and mental. More recent forms of dualism tend to let go of the idea of substance, and focus on properties. In other words, there are different levels at which a complex entity can be considered and described. Mental properties are applied to a level of complexity – i.e. the workings of a complex being as a whole, as opposed to the workings of the individual parts that make it up – that is quite different from that to which physical properties apply. Thus we have a *property dualism* – the same complex physical thing having two very different sets of properties, with mental properties not reducible to physical ones.

One of the problems with this idea – both in Spinoza's approach, and in modern property dualism – is that, if mental attributes are applied to the same reality as physical attributes, then it would seem that causality, which appears to determine all that happens in the physical world, will therefore remove all freedom from intelligent human action. Freedom becomes an illusion.

### COMMENT

There are two modern developments in connection with dualism that will be considered later in this chapter. One is the criticism of Descartes offered by Ryle, based on a linguistic approach. The other is the consideration of the way in which qualities can be applied to complex entities, in terms of 'supervenience'. But before considering these, it is necessary to examine the two alternatives to dualism: materialism and idealism.

# Materialism and behaviourism

'I am body and soul' – so speaks the child. And why should one not speak like children?

But the Awakened, the enlightened man says: I am body entirely, and nothing beside; and soul is only a word for something in the body.

The Body is a great intelligence, a multiplicity with one sense, a war and a peace, a herd and a herdsman.

Your little intelligence, my brother, which you call 'spirit', is also the instrument of your body, a little instrument and toy of your great intelligence.

You say 'I' and you are proud of this word. But greater than this – although you will not believe it – is your body and its great intelligence, which does not say 'I' but performs 'I'.

(*Thus Spoke Zarathustra*, Nietzsche)

In many areas of philosophy, religion and politics, Nietzsche (1844–1900) anticipated later debates and that is, in part, why he is one of the most fascinating thinkers of the 19th Century. His comments that opened this section are from part of *Zarathustra* entitled 'On the despisers of the body'. In this section he appears to be attacking those who hold a dualistic position for primarily religious reasons and who therefore tend to demote the body.

He anticipates behaviourism and the linguistic analysis of language about the self, by saying that the soul is 'only a word for something in the body' and also brings together more recent thinking about the role of the mind and its relationship with emotions and those drives that are based on the promptings of hormones, by pointing out that the mind is both 'herd and herdsman'. In other words, in some way the mind embraces all the dynamic elements within the body, but also has the role of controlling and directing them. His idea of the 'great intelligence' therefore appears to embrace both rationality and emotion, both conscious and unconscious. It is not merely the self that identifies itself as 'I', but the 'I' that operates as an independent entity. We shall return to this later, in considering the instrumentalist approach to mind.

In this section, we shall be looking at some approaches which, like Nietzsche's, set aside the dualism of Descartes by eliminating the need for a separate mental substance – seeing the mind as a feature of the body and language about the mind as being a convenient way of describing actual or anticipated bodily actions.

In general, therefore, a materialism approach is one that claims that mental phenomena can be explained in terms of, or reduced to, physical phenomena.

---

**'is'**

In any situation where two things – in the case of materialism, thought and brain processes – are identified, it is important to distinguish between the 'is' of definition and the 'is' of composition. Thus, for example, a symphony 'is' merely a set of vibrations in the air. It is *composed of* those vibrations and without those vibrations, no symphony. Of course, the meaning of 'vibrations in the air' and 'symphony' are quite different. The symphony cannot sensibly be *defined as* vibrations in the air, even if it is composed of them.

As we progress through various theories, we need to be aware that some of the objections that are raised to a materialist view are based on the assumption that once you have an identity of composition, it automatically follows that you have an identity of definition.

In other words, if my thoughts are 'nothing but' brain processes (in the sense of being composed of those and no other phenomena), then it follows that thoughts are 'the same thing as' brain processes, which is obvious nonsense. What happens in the grey matter between our ears is nothing like the sensations of colour or sound, or the emotions and thoughts that are experienced.

---

Thomas Hobbes (1588–1679) was concerned to understand the nature of perception. He argued that external objects exerted physical pressure on our sense organs and that these physical effects were mediated by nerves to the mind and heart. There they take on the appearance of being qualities in the external body. But Hobbes holds that they are in fact a matter of *fancy*; in other words, that they are mental constructs. And he holds that this must be the case, since physical movement can only cause other physical movement.

Hence, whatever causes sense experience, causes only physical activity; it cannot cause what we experience as sensations, which are clearly non-physical. Thus, although we think that our concept (fancy) actually applies to the external object, nevertheless the object is one thing, the image or fancy is another.

In a sense, this leads Hobbes to the kind of 'internal theatre' view of the mind, although he also makes the distinction between the mind that assembles such 'fancies' and the physical basis of consciousness, which is part of an ongoing chain of physical causes and effects.

For Hobbes therefore, even perception is part of the mechanical, physical world, and – rather like the epiphenomenal approach – what we term 'mind' builds on it. And, of course, with the triumph of Newtonian science, everything came to be seen in terms of the interaction of physical bodies, moved by forces that operated in terms of the laws of physics.

A materialist approach need not deny that there are mental states, it simply says that to have a mental state is simply what happens when a particular brain state is taking place. So, to take the most common example, feeling a pain is a real, conscious experience – but it is simply what happens when there is a certain pattern of activity in your brain and nervous system.

However, there is good evidence to suggest that the mind is, in

### A challenge

Sit down, shut your eyes and try to become conscious of what it means to say that consciousness does not exist!

You cannot succeed in that process, any more than Descartes could doubt that he was a thinking being or David Hume (1711–1776) could be aware without being aware *of* something or other – for, like Hobbes, he had a 'theatre' view of the mind,

> aware always of a procession of images and thoughts. And the reason: nobody can doubt that thinking or awareness is *an experienced process*. The question that dominates the mind/body issue is whether that experienced process has a particular physical origin, whether it is (in some sense) a substance, how it relates to the physical world and whether it can *do* anything.

some way, just a feature of the brain. For example, a person suffering severe depression can be helped by having ECT treatment, which involves giving the brain electric shocks, simulating epileptic fits. Equally, a person who suffers brain damage may become a changed character. It is also possible to monitor every human activity in terms of physical movements brought about by electro-chemical activity in muscles, nerves and brain. It can always be seen as a self-contained electro-mechanical process, with no 'gap' requiring the intervention of the mind. But, if there seems no point at which the mind intervenes in that chain of causes, why do we need to think in terms of a mind at all?

In general, materialism takes a reductionist approach to mental activity; a person is seen as 'nothing but' a brain, attached to a body and nervous system. The 'nothing but' distinguishes materialism from more subtle forms of dualism. Nobody would deny that, in some sense, a mind is closely linked to a brain and nervous system; the problem is to express what a 'something more' might be, if the materialist position seems inadequate. Notice that most materialists do not want to say that mental states do not exist, they simply say that they are nothing other than brain states. In other words, they do not accept some secondary mental 'substance' of the sort that Descartes accepted.

Even if the materialist position is correct and the mind is nothing other than the physical activity of the brain, that need not hinder the examination of 'mental' concepts. In other words, it is quite unreasonable to abandon speaking about the mind, just because we know it to be the firing of neurones in the brain, any more than we would be tempted to stop speaking about Mozart simply because we know his music is nothing by vibrations in the air.

## Behaviourism

Behaviourism is a materialist theory, in that it reduces 'mental' concepts, such as having a pain or being happy, to physical activity. For a behaviourist, crying out and rubbing the damaged part of the body is exactly what 'being in pain' is about. There is no separate or private activity going on, over and above the physical and publicly observable behaviour. In psychology, behaviourism developed out of the frustration of trying to find something that could be observed and monitored (as opposed to sensations which were only known through introspection and evidence for which could not be assessed objectively) and became an important feature of 20th-Century psychological investigation.

Pavlov (1849–1936) in Russia, J. B. Watson (1875–1958) and Fred Skinner (1904–1990) in the USA were hugely influential in their day. Their work was based on measuring physical responses to stimuli. Indeed, the term 'Pavlovian reaction' is commonly used to describe an immediate and 'unthinking' response.

### Example

Pavlov, for example, would monitor a dog's salivation at the sight or anticipation of food and then explore ways in which it might be trained to expect food if it performed a particular action. Behaviourists generally worked in labs, watching the way in which animals learned to do simple tasks, such as pressing a switch in the hope of getting food.

---

**KEY POINT**

Behaviourism describes and specifies, but it does not explain.

---

This approach to studying the mind may seem very limited, considering the range of views that we have considered so far, but one should keep in mind that the aim of behaviourism was to produce a science of mind, with results that could be measured and evaluated; the measurement of behaviour in response to stimuli representing the only such measurable data – so it was quite natural that behaviour should be seen as the key to finding out what was happening in the mind. The issue, of course, was whether, having found such responses to stimuli, you had thereby adequately explained what it meant by mental activity.

In general, the behaviourists saw the task of psychology as predicting and controlling behaviour, but the environment shaped that behaviour. Our activity is not decided by some private activity going on in the mind, but by our conditioned responses to the environment.

---

**COMMENT**

There is an important political agenda here. A behaviourist approach considers people to be shaped primarily by their environment, they are simply responding to their circumstances. By contrast, a dualist may hold that the mind is distinct from the body and is able to control what the body does. A behaviourist is more likely to consider people as products of their particular background, class and so on. A dualist is more likely to see an individual as unique and as potentially able to transcend his or her circumstances.

The behaviourist approach seemed to offer a scientific basis for psychology, but also had enormous implications for sociology and education. If minds were simply responses to stimuli, then control of the content of education would be a key feature in shaping people's lives. It was not just that minds could be controlled, but that minds were the product of conditioning and whoever controls that conditioning, controls everything.

It is almost impossible to overemphasise the importance of this distinction between dualism and behaviourism – so much in terms of the politics, the philosophy and the culture of the 20th Century was shaped by what was, in effect, the issue about whether individuals have unique, independent minds or are the products of conditioning.

Behaviourism was interesting in terms of understanding the basis of learning, but it made no reference to any subjective activity. This approach is still used today in treating phobias, for example, but otherwise behaviourism is very much a thing of the past. The latter part of the 20th Century saw what might be termed 'the cognitive revolution' in which the whole emphasis in psychology and the philosophy of mind shifted towards issues of consciousness and an examination of the mind in terms of its *function*, what role it plays in the way we live.

---

**COMMENT**

The key question, when making the move towards modern cognitive science from the older behaviourist approach is simply this:

How do you move from the examination of physical phenomena, in terms of brain activity and conditioned responses, to an appreciation of the *whole* phenomenon we know as subjectivity?

---

The behaviourist's dilemma:

- You can't observe thought.
- Therefore any one account of the thought that gave rise to an action is as good as any other, since it is not open to verification of any sort.
- The behaviourist answer is to ignore thought and go for what can be observed – behaviour.
- But human behaviour is so complex and so obviously related to overall views and goals, that it is impossible to give an adequate description of it (let alone an explanation) without bringing in some idea of the workings of the mind.

## Example

A person steps off the pavement and holds up their hand to stop the traffic. An oncoming vehicle stops, allowing a car to back out of a concealed drive into the road. The person then waves the vehicle on and mouths the word 'Thanks' to the driver:

- It is almost inconceivable that the ability to perform those actions could have been learned by trial and error! (How many times would he get knocked down before it works?)
- It is possible that the person who stopped the car has never had to do so before, neither has the person ever had to back out of that drive into the road before.
- Stopping one's car when a person holds up their hand is straightforward – a rule to be learned.
- By the same token, what of the sequence in which a person recognises that it is a difficult turning to back out of; thinks that there is a danger of a collision; decides to go and stop the traffic; beckons the car out; acknowledges and thanks the driver who has stopped? Could each of these have been learned by a process of stimulus and response?
- Is it not more likely that there is a sequence of private 'thoughts' imagining various scenarios and working out which of these are desirable (a safe journey) or not (getting hit when backing out) and then working out what needs to be done to secure the first rather than the second?
- It may be possible that basic behaviourism could go a long way to showing the stimulus and response basis for all that action. But the result would be very complex indeed. It is easier to posit some form of mental activity, even if it cannot be observed directly.

In general, we need to distinguish two kinds of behaviourism. The approach described just may be termed *methodological behaviourism*, in that it simply relates input stimuli to the resulting behaviour. *Logical behaviourism* takes this a step further, suggesting that mental terms can be defined in terms of observable behaviour. For example, to have a pain *means* to grimace, clutch the affected spot and so on. The best-known exponent of this approach is Gilbert Ryle (see page 37).

## Eliminative materialism

This approach, taken by the American philosopher Richard Rorty (b. 1931) and others, makes what appears to be the implausible claim that mental states simply do not exist. When we speak of mental phenomena – thoughts, desires, emotions and so on – there is nothing that corresponds to those words *other than physical states*.

The argument goes that, were it possible to give a complete account of brain activity (in other words a perfect neurobiology), we would have a complete explanation of brain functioning and there would be no place within that explanation for things like beliefs or hopes.

---

**COMMENT**

John Searle, in *The Rediscovery of Mind*, criticises this approach. He argues that it is the equivalent of saying that a perfect theory of nuclear physics could explain all reality and therefore that ordinary objects, like cars and golf clubs, do not exist!

---

Another significant aspect of eliminative materialism is that it is 'anti-foundationalist'; in other words, it argues that there is nothing inside us that we have not put there ourselves and no fundamental principle of reason that is not simply a convention that we have chosen to use. In other words, there are no transcendent or general foundations for 'mind', but merely the gathering together of what society offers.

It may be worth reflecting on this alongside the views of postmodernists on what others would think of as the creative artist or author. Just as postmodernist approaches tend to edge out the creative self, in favour of seeing creativity in terms of the gathering of already existing and socially defined material, so eliminative materialism edges out any sense of a mind that can be described in terms other than those applying to brain processes.

# Idealism

At the opposite extreme to materialism is the less popular view that the fundamental reality is mind – that everything we experience of the physical world is simply an experience and is therefore mediated through mind. It makes no sense to say that something exists independent of my (or someone's) experience of it, because there is no way to know anything exists except as an experience in a mind. The best-known exponent of this position is George Berkeley (1685–1753).

Physical objects, on Berkeley's reckoning, are no different from the sense impression that we have of them. In other words, we do not have a problem of asking how our image of the world compares with the world itself – because *it is* the world itself, as far as we are concerned.

He therefore points out that our thoughts and the things we imagine cannot take place without a mind to think or imagine them and he therefore argues (in *The Principles of Human Knowledge*) that the various sensations which, combined, are the way we understand the world, are also dependent on the perceiving mind.

---

**IN OTHER WORDS**

To use Berkeley's own example, I can say that the table on which I write exists, because I can see and feel it. If out of the room, I can still say that the table exists, meaning that, if I or anyone else were to enter the room, he or she would perceive it. It therefore makes no sense to say that it exists, except in the context of being perceived.

---

'To be is to be perceived' is the key to his approach; to be perceived with the qualities that our senses give something is what it means to say that something exists. What is fascinating about Berkeley's argument is how close it comes to the position of a very different group of philosophers – the 20th-Century logical positivists. They, too, held that meaningful language had to be backed up by sense experience. What Berkeley accepted, but they did not, was that things continued to exist between being perceived by individuals, because they were constantly being perceived by God.

Descartes had argued that the senses could be deceived and hence – like the physical body – they are on the side of those things of which he cannot be certain. Descartes' self is simply a *thinking* thing, quite separate from perceptions. For Berkeley, the point of certainty seems to have shifted towards perceptions. The world itself is only known through the minds of thinking things that perceive it.

Whereas materialists see the body as certain and mind as a way of describing physical actions and dispositions, idealists see the mind and its perceptions as certain and the external world as an assumption we make on the basis of them.

---

**COMMENT**

Berkeley's views are sometimes portrayed as quite unreasonable and as going against common sense. In fact, his argument – that we can have no knowledge of the external world that is independent of our sensations (and thus of our mental activity) – has considerable force.

To experience the strength of this argument, just look around you for a moment, keeping your head quite still. Be aware of colours, shapes, perhaps the touch of things close to you. See all these things as 'out there', beyond that great window between your ears through which you experience your vision of the world. Then close one eye and gently press on one side of your other eyeball. Everything you see shifts a little. Hold that for a moment. Can you tell that it shifted? Touch something and your experience of touch exactly matches your 'shifted' vision, as though giving confirmation that the shifted vision is in fact correct. Remove the pressure on the eyeball; the world shifts back to 'normal', and your touch confirmed *that* view as well. Imaginatively enter into the sense that there is an 'internal theatre' which you actually experience as the external world.

If it illustrates nothing else, this shows the extent to which the mind organises the sensations it receives and compensates for any mismatch in the information. If it did not, then your sense of touch would not have been experienced as exactly corresponding to your 'shifted' vision.

That may not lead you to say that the external world does not exist, but it is a reminder that the very solid 'external' world is, in reality, a mental construct, formed as your brain synthesises the sense impressions it receives.

John Locke (1632–1710) had distinguished between primary qualities (e.g. physical dimensions), which belonged to objects quite independent of our perception of them, and secondary qualities (e.g. colour, smell), which were clearly linked to our sensations. Science, of course, was concerned with the former, personal experience with the latter. The implication of the idealist approach is that the only thing of which we can be certain is our own mind and the sensations it receives. The problem is not that the mind may be unreal, but that – for all we know – it is the physical world that may be unreal. Without our own judgement, sorting out the perceptions that come via our senses, we would know nothing. Until the 20th Century, such views seemed to go against the apparently objective certainties of science and were therefore less popular. Over the last 100 years or so, it has become increasingly recognised that even in our scientific investigations, we influence what we examine and that the mind plays a creative role. Not, of course, that the world does not exist, but that it cannot be known to exist except in relationship to the way in which minds perceive it.

# The Ghost in the Machine

*The Concept of Mind* (1949) by Gilbert Ryle was an enormously influential book. It applied a linguistic approach to philosophy and (which was of growing significance for philosophy at that time) to the issues of mind. In other words, it was concerned with concepts and their meaning – asking questions such as 'What does it mean to call an action intelligent?'.

Ryle suggested that to speak of minds and bodies as though they were equivalent things was to make a 'category mistake'. So, to use one of his own examples:

> A foreigner watching his first game of cricket learns what are the functions of the bowlers, the batsmen, the fielders, the umpires and the scorers. He then says 'But there is no one left on the field to contribute the famous element of team-spirit. I see who does the bowling, the batting and the wicket-keeping; but I do not see whose role it is to exercise *esprit de corps*?'

Clearly, the term 'esprit de corps' is used to describe the way in which all this is done, but it is not identified with any one distinct function. Similarly, therefore, he argues that 'mind' does not describe something over and above the various physical actions that intelligent beings carry out, it simply describes them as intelligent. To see a 'mental' activity as taking place alongside various physical activities is to commit a category mistake:

> My destructive purpose is to show that a family of radical category-mistakes is the source of the double-life theory. The representation of a person as a ghost mysteriously ensconced in a machine derives from this argument.

Essentially, the mind/body problem is shifted for Ryle. Instead of asking how we know that physical behaviour is influenced by some other, non-physical system, known as the mind, the task he sets himself is to define what sort of criteria can be used to decide if, for example, the adjective or adverb 'intelligent' has been correctly ascribed.

Ryle's target is what he called the 'official' view, stemming from Descartes, which he calls the doctrine of the 'Ghost in the Machine'. He says of it:

> It maintains that there exist both bodies and minds; that there occur physical processes and mental processes; that there are mechanical causes of corporeal movements and mental causes of corporeal movements. I shall argue that these and

other analogous conjunctions are absurd; but, it must be noticed, the argument will not show that either of the illegitimately conjoined propositions is absurd in itself. I am not, for example, denying that there occur mental processes. Doing long division is a mental process and so is making a joke. But I am saying that the phrase 'there occur mental processes' does not mean the same sort of thing as 'there occur physical processes', and, therefore, that it makes no sense to conjoin or disjoin the two.

Ryle therefore wants to say that mental descriptions (e.g. 'intelligent') are simply ways of describing particular kinds of physical activity. I cannot look inside a person's mind and see their intelligence, I infer it from what they say and do. In other words, I can have 'mind talk', without having to accept the existence of a separate substance called 'mind'.

A key feature of Ryle's view is that it is a mistake to say that *your mind* did something; rather you should simply say that *you* did it. In other words, Ryle argued that to say a person was kind was not describing a quality in some unknown 'mind', but simply describing a feature of the attitudes and behaviour of that person. Mental predicates apply to a person, not to something called his or her 'mind'.

---

**COMMENT**

In terms of the meaning and verification of the words we use, Ryle's argument is a powerful one. If I say 'I was unkind', I am describing a mental quality, but also a particular physical expression of that quality. Thus, if asked 'In what way?' I would describe actions done or words said that caused hurt.

Now the meaning of the word 'unkind' is a public one – if it were not, then nobody would understand what it meant. Thus, to describe a personal attitude or feeling, one has to use images and concepts that are in the public domain. Words do not 'mean' unless they mean something that is in the public domain.

There are two important things to be distinguished here. It is one thing to say that the concept of mind is in a way redundant, and that one can simply apply mental predicates directly to a person; but it is another to say that those mental predicates can be identified with the physical expression that they describe.

### Example

You see an actress express a whole range of emotions on stage. You see her angry, sad or elated. There need be no doubt in your mind what emotion is being shown, it is clear. Now, we have no privileged access to the actress's mind. We simply see what she shows and she shows those emotions by imaginatively entering into the drama that has been scripted for her. So far, so Ryle – no problem. But we know that the emotions are not those of the actor herself, only of the part she is playing.

If the actions and gestures were taken as *identical* to the emotions, then the actress would indeed suffer bereavement, elation or whatever every time she went on stage. That cannot be the case. Deception and play acting are only possible because we habitually use physical actions, words and gestures to indicate what a person thinks and feels. We may be deceived – and deception requires that there is something which is hidden from us, namely whether the external appearances do, in fact, depict what that person is thinking and feeling.

One of the problems with Ryle's approach is that, because it equates a mental state with a physical disposition, it is difficult to take into account the influence of one mental state on another. And yet we are all the time open to many different (and sometimes conflicting) desires and beliefs, which influence how we behave.

For example, someone on hunger strike is offered food. He refuses it. If the mental experience of hunger is defined as the desire to eat food, then at that moment the hunger striker is not hungry. But that is crazy: he is hungry, but refuses food on principle. It is difficult to see how such internal debates, overriding expected activity, can be accounted for if all mental states are ultimately reduced to actions and dispositions to act.

Ultimately, Ryle seems to mistake the *criteria* for describing a mental state with the description itself. It may indeed be true that, from a narrow view of language as having meaning only if it can be shown to correspond to externally perceived events and entities, mental predicates depend on observing certain forms of behaviour, but that is certainly not the basis on which I ascribe them in the case of my own experiences.

---

**COMMENT**

One wonders just how worldly wise some philosophers are. Have they never played games of bluff or tried to fool opponents into thinking that they have a better set of cards in their hand than is actually the case? Have they never tried to appear stern, while suppressing hilarity, in reprimanding a child who has done something outlandishly naughty? Have they never deceived, even just a little, in the game of love?

In the real world, thoughts, feelings, hopes, desires and all the deviousness of a mind that seeks its own ends come first and actions follow. That is the way human beings operate. They also become adept at watching for the gullible, interpreting body language and generally trying to get ahead in the game of guessing what others are thinking and feeling.

---

## Interpreting action

Ryle suggests that we can apply mental predicates to physical actions – i.e. that an action is 'clever'. Mental descriptions are generally statements about dispositions to act in a particular way. The problem is that, when we come to describe action, we are actually interpreting, rather than describing what we see. The ascriptions 'clever' or 'cunning', for example, do not refer to the particular action, but to an interpretation of the significance of that action in its context. The action becomes cunning, because it is clearly part of a strategy, aimed at some future goal.

But here we hit a problem, for the interpretation presupposes exactly what Ryle wants to avoid. 'Cunning' does describe the action, but not simply its physical attributes. Another person might do exactly the same thing and yet not be described as cunning. Cunning presupposes forethought, planning, means and ends – in other words, mental operations, the very things that Ryle says we cannot describe.

It is a key feature of experience that we always experience things 'as' something and that 'as' is an interpretation and thus a feature contributed by our mind. Our senses may register a blob of red with a distinctive scent; our mind registers 'rose'. All descriptions of physical behaviour, far from being 'all there is' when it comes to describing another person, require the idea of mind to make sense of them.

## A 'place' for mind?

It is clear that Ryle will not accept anything that sets mental and physical attributes alongside one another as though they belonged to the same category – and he accuses the traditional Cartesian dualist position of doing just that. But there are two important points to make about his criticism:

1  It is possible to be a dualist without holding, as Descartes did, that the mind is completely separate and distinct from the body, with the one physical and extended and the other not. It is possible to have a dualism of qualities, rather than of substances. In other words, you could see a human being as a physical structure, but one that has two sets of properties. One set comprises physical data, colour of hair, colour of eyes, height, weight and so on. The other comprises mental qualities: kind, selfish, thoughtful, irritable, experiencing pain or unhappiness. These refer to the same entity, but they are non-physical qualities that describe how that living organism relates to its stimuli and – in a sense – how it feels. Such non-physical qualities may be known through observation (I see someone running down the street with a broad grin on his or her face) or through the sharing of language (someone complains of pain and I know what that word means and can imaginatively enter into his or her situation because I have experienced similar things

myself). Hence, I am not learning about some 'other' person, separate from the physical entity I see before me. Rather, I see that person in a particular way, in terms of his or her response and communication – that is what yields the non-physical characteristics.

2 Descartes was not as simplistic as Ryle makes out. In saying that the mind is unextended, he implies that the mind does not exist in the same sense that physical things exist. It cannot operate alongside physical causes, because it does not have a place within that empirical world. Mental events do not happen 'alongside' physical ones. But once that is taken into account, the thrust of Ryle's criticism of dualism is effectively the same one that has been raised all along – namely that, given that the physical world offers a seamless network of causes, it is not possible to specify in what way mind makes a difference, since all difference making is automatically assumed to be accounted for by some physical cause, whether known or unknown.

## Supervenience

In the world of Cartesian dualism, there are physical things and there are mental things. The two are distinct, separate substances and each appears to be able to exist without the other. On the one hand, one can explore in the physical world and find no trace of mind. Thus the materialist will, in order to explain mind, have to find something – brain activity or behaviour – to explain it. Mind is just a way of talking about physical things. On the other hand, the idealist points out that all we can know about are the contents of our minds – the physical world is constructed out of our ideas. And it is no good common sense trying to claim that we all know the physical world is out there really, because we cannot say what that means without using still more ideas!

Hence the game is played out with two circles, which do not appear to meet, but which clearly influence one another. Life makes no sense without both the physical and the mental; that much is clear.

A more recent view of the world (and this has partly come about as the result of the rise of cognitive science, as we shall see in the next chapter) is not dualist but multi-layered.

In part, this follows from the older reductionist approach. A complex organism can be reduced to its component parts and those parts reduced still further and so on. The temptation earlier was to say that the complex organism was, in fact 'nothing but' the sum total of all those constituent parts into which it had been reduced.

That same image can now be viewed differently. As simple things gather together to form more complex units, so those units appear to have qualities that were not there in the simpler parts. Thus chemicals take on qualities that are not seen in atoms and cells take on qualities not seen in their constituent chemicals. The further up the chain of complexity you go, the more qualities emerge that were not seen lower down.

So, in terms of biology, once you get to have individual living cells, they have the ability to take in nourishment and to reproduce. Life thus *emerges* from its constituent parts. Being a 'living thing' means something – to be able to reproduce, for example – that is real, but which cannot be true of the simpler chemicals of which the cell is composed.

Taking that a stage further, a human being has what we call consciousness. We can think, choose, respond creatively to situations, experience emotions and decide how to act. But the various cells that make up our bodies do not have those qualities or abilities: consciousness, or the mental world, has emerged once life gets to a certain level of complexity.

We have two terms that are used in modern discussion to cover that situation: *emergence* and *supervenience*.

Emergence has been described already. Supervenience is used for this process in that mental properties *supervene* on physical ones. The mental description does not have to refer to something else, in some other place. It is about the same physical phenomenon as the ordinary physical description, but it describes the situation from a 'higher' or more complex level.

Now, this multi-level approach to reality leads us to use a third term – *realisation*. If mental properties supervene on physical ones, then it would seem possible that the same mental property could come about in connection with different physical bases. In other words, it might be possible to see a mental quality being realised in the physical arrangement of neurones firing in the human brain, but also in a computer memory. This creates all sorts of other problems, which we shall start to look at in the next chapter.

One result of this change of view is the return to a consideration of *consciousness*. If consciousness emerges at a particular level of complexity, can it emerge in anything that has the required complexity? Is it inevitable that computers, as they become more powerful, will eventually take on what we call consciousness?

The real problem with this approach is to know why it is that activity at one level gives rise to activity at another. Why is it that 'pleasure' supervenes on one set of physical stimuli and 'pain' on another? Just what mechanism is that that can connect these different layers?

If *multiple realisations* are possible – for example, in a brain and in a computer – this has a very clear implication for the reductionist approach to mind. An old-fashioned reductionist is going to claim that the mental phenomenon is 'nothing but' the physical activity which brings it about. A feeling of being in love is 'nothing but' the action of hormones!

If that same mental property can be brought about by ('realised in') different physical arrangements, it cannot be identified with any one of them; it must include but go beyond them. In other words, it needs to be considered functionally, not in terms of a fixed thing or essence.

---

**FOR REFLECTION**

This may also have implication for our understanding of the personality traits displayed by animals. If an emotion has to be realised in one particular physical form – the human brain – then animals may have similar but not identical emotions. If, by the same token, an emotion (e.g. friendliness) can be realised in the physical makeup of both animals and humans, then we are sharing exactly the same emotion. Of course, not all friendliness is the same (the dog that comes up to lick me may be genetically programmed to do so in a way that I am not), but that can be a difference between human individuals as well as between humans and other species. You may not know why a dog behaves in that way, but you probably don't know why I do either!

But if multiple realisations are possible, then what the dog feels in terms of happiness or the desire to welcome someone familiar may be exactly the same as what I feel.

Just as we find that the same basic elements throughout the universe – water and ice will be the same, even if found on a distant planet – so elements of consciousness need not be limited to the human realm, but may be realised in many different species.

This leads on to functionalism, in which a mental property is considered as the causal link between some input stimulus and the resulting response, and which may therefore perform the same task in very different realisations. This we shall consider at the end of the next chapter (Cognitive Science), since it is an approach that has developed along with that broader range of disciplines.

We can note here, however, that the idea of multiple realisations is not really a new one. Aristotle recognised that the form of something could be realised in many different material examples. Thus, when he categorised things, the category included many physical differences. So, for example, 'cat' is a form, but it is realised in many different shapes and colours of moggy! If we see form as the essential structure of a thing, then there is no reason why the essential structure and function of something mental cannot be found in many different physical forms.

# A new approach

Up to the middle of the 20th Century, work in this field was polarised. There were those, on the one hand, who took a behaviourist or materialist approach – psychologists like Skinner examined the behaviour of rats, philosophers like Quine and Ryle saw mental qualities as describing features of our physical behaviour. On the other hand, there were those, particularly from a religious point of view, who were adamant that the mind or soul should remain distinct from the body.

However, in the final decades of the 20th Century, there arose a renewed interest in the mind and a recognition that something more was going on than could be accounted for on a behaviourist basis, and which (as we have seen) raised many philosophical questions – without necessarily going in for the straightforward dualism that had been around since the time of Descartes.

It was also widely recognised that the Cartesian division of reality into material substances and mental substances was fundamentally flawed and that there was no need to hold a dualist, materialist or even one of the intermediate positions – all of which depended to some extent on an acceptance of the parameters set out by Descartes.

Then, in the 1970s – as we shall see in the next chapter – there developed what amounted to a new field of study, cognitive science, as developments in psychology, linguistics, computing and information technology came to bear on the traditional philosophical problem of mind.

# 3 | COGNITIVE SCIENCE

In turning to modern cognitive science, let us be clear about why this represents an entirely new approach to the philosophy of mind. We saw in the last chapter that Descartes' radical dualism of body and mind dominated the thinking in this area until the middle of the 20th Century. Even those (like the logical positivists or Ryle) who dismissed talk of minds as being either meaningless or as covert ways of speaking about physical actions or appearances, were nevertheless under the spell of the Cartesian view that the mind was, in some way, completely different from, and external to, the physical realm.

Dualists struggled to understand how the mental could influence the physical and vice versa, since there seemed to be no mechanism that could span the gulf between mental and physical. Behaviourists and materialists simply regarded the mental as a mistaken (even if convenient) way of speaking about collections of physical phenomena.

By the 1950s the problems in the philosophy of mind seemed straightforward, if insoluble. On the one hand, there was the whole raft of problems associated with the impossibility of perceiving mental events (other than one's own, through introspection) – knowledge of other minds, how the mind could be said to affect the body and vice versa. On the other, there were debates about the status and verifiability (or otherwise) of language about minds and mental events – typified by Ryle's challenge to Cartesian dualism.

In a sense, the philosophical debates about mind became blocked at that level. Few doubted the phenomenon of mind – for, like Descartes, the act of doubting was itself seen as mental. Yet it was difficult to see how the dualistic gulf could be bridged and how the mental could be examined in empirical and scientific terms.

Into this situation there came new academic disciplines.

- ■ Linguistics was a development of the philosophy of language, seeking to use a scientific approach to issues of communication.
- ■ The rapid development of computers raised issues of whether it might be possible to construct a machine that could imitate the process of thought – or indeed, whether such a machine could be considered to be 'thinking'.
- ■ Neuroscience and pharmacology were also examining the nature and working of the human brain and the effect of drugs on behaviour and 'mental' states.
- ■ Clinical psychology had a contribution to make, since it considered the mind in terms of its function (both conscious and unconscious) in the life of the individual, rather than simply taking a behaviourist approach.

It was clear that the philosophy of mind could not long stand aloof from these allied disciplines, since they were covering very similar territory but from different (and largely scientific) starting points. Hence the term 'cognitive science' was developed, to indicate an interdisciplinary area of study concerned both with the process of human cognition (the theory of knowledge, that had previously been described as 'epistemology' in traditional philosophy) and issues connected to the brain and its relationship to thought, activity and communication.

Cognitive science therefore presents itself as an interdisciplinary and scientifically based approach to many of the issues traditionally considered under the philosophy of mind. It takes an approach that includes scientific experiment and evidence, rather than being limited to the traditional philosophical process of reflection, introspection and the analysis of language.

One thing to keep in mind, as we look at this broad approach, is that the early development of cognitive science still followed the earlier behaviourists in that they studied *observable phenomena*. The difference between cognitive science and behaviourism was the range of phenomena that were taken into consideration. As we shall see later in this chapter, the functionalist approach to the mind saw mental events and qualities as possibly expressed through a variety of different physical states (much as the a piece of computer software can run on different hardware) – so it became theoretically possible to study mental phenomena without needing to have an exhaustive knowledge of the brain or the workings of a computer memory chip. What mattered was the *function* of the mental quality and this was largely independent of the physical environment in which it was operating. This tied in well with the development of artificial intelligence, since 'mental' phenomena were functions that could be performed in a simple way by computers as well as by human brains.

**Note**

In Chapter 8, we shall be considering consciousness, looking at the subjective, internal aspects of experience – what it means to experience things as having particular colours, sounds, tastes and so on. This is the *phenomenal* approach to the mind; looking at the phenomena of experience.

In cognitive science, there is another approach. Following the earlier work of behaviourists, it is concerned with what the mind *does*. In other words, it examines the physical activity that results from mental activity. It examines the mind in terms of its causal effects. This *psychological* approach reflects the workings of the mind and its impact, rather than the experience of actually being a conscious, intelligent being.

In short: consciousness considers what the mind feels like; cognitive science considers what it does. This distinction is set out very clearly by David Chalmers in *The Conscious Mind* (1996).

## Psychology

The functionalist approach to mind is also illustrated by the development of psychology as a science. The early 'structuralists' attempted to analyse all experience into its component sensations. So Wundt and others, working in the 1870s, hoped to discover the workings of the mind by asking subjects to reflect on their experience and report back on it. In this way they built up a detailed pattern for analysing experience. By doing this, however, they generally blurred a distinction between looking at what the mind does and the reporting of the experiences of the mind. It was assumed that such detailed reporting was the only way to get information about the mind. In the end, this approach failed, since they had no means of knowing whether the reporting was accurate, as there was no way of checking sensations objectively.

In 1890 William James, who was for many years Professor of Psychology at Harvard, wrote *Principles of Psychology*, which became the standard textbook; two years later he wrote *Psychology: The Briefer Course*. In these books, he looked at the function of the emotions and the way in which people can give physical expression to them. In particular, he suggested that emotions (or passions) could be cultivated by adopting the appropriate physical postures associated with them. (To put this crudely: look good and you'll feel good; wave your fist in the air and courage will arise in you.) He thought that the reverse was also true, that if you simply refused to give any physical expression to an emotion, it would die.

In terms of the philosophy of mind, this view has two significant implications:

- ■ That there is a constant two-way process of influence going on between minds and bodies; it is not simply that the mind controls the body.
- ■ That mental activity (expressing emotions or passions) can be assessed by its method of expression – i.e. the physical activity to which it gives rise. (It became a relatively short step from that point to saying that waving one's fist is what 'being angry' really means – the view taken by Ryle, see pages 38–9.)

At the same time, Freud was developing his theory about the effect of the unconscious mind on the behaviour and attitudes of neurotic patients. In terms of the philosophy of mind, this illustrated that the mind (particularly the unconscious) could have a most profound effect on a person's well-being, without that person being able even to identify the root cause of his or her problems.

In a totally different direction, we have already mentioned (see page 30) the behaviourist tradition. In psychology, this is found particularly from the work of Pavlov (in Russia) and Skinner (in the USA) and it was typified by the testing out of animals in controlled conditions, examining their responses to stimuli and their adopting of habitual patterns in order to make sense of their experience. Notice that this approach had no need to posit internal, conscious mental states at all, all that was required was to measure stimulus and response. The 'internal' aspect was irrelevant to what was being examined. A common feature of psychological approaches, however, was that they were considering the way the mind functions in the life of an individual. Whether it was the effect that, for example, trauma in early childhood could have later in life or the way in which a rat could learn to perform a simple operation in order to get more food, the mind was functioning. It was not a matter of debating whether minds existed, but exploring how they did what they did. This was in line with the increasingly 'functionalist' views of the mind that were emerging as a result of the study of artificial intelligence.

# Language and innate knowledge

Innate knowledge is an interesting touchstone for evaluating different theories of mind. There is a fundamental difference of approach between rationalists (e.g. Descartes) and empiricists (e.g. Hobbes or Locke). Those who take a rationalist approach may hold the view that some ideas are innate. In other words, that we are all born with a set of fundamental ideas and ways of thinking and that it is only through these that we can understand the world as we do. This approach goes back to Plato, where we only know individual things because we have prior knowledge of the eternal 'forms'. Indeed, Plato considered that true knowledge (as opposed to opinion) could not come through the senses, since they were always fallible.

Contrariwise, those who took the empiricist approach (that all knowledge comes through sense experience) were able to say that people have innate *capabilities* – in other words, that they are born with the ability to do certain things, including certain mental operations. What they cannot have (in the absence of empirical evidence provided by the senses) is innate *knowledge*.

## Chomsky

Naom Chomsky (b.1928) made a case for innate capabilities, in terms of the acquisition of language. He argued that children do not gradually learn the grammar of a language before they start to speak it. Rather, they seem to know how to put words together – that they have an innate sense of how language works. In other words, everyone is biologically programmed to speak a language.

In favour of this view was the fact that very different languages have deep structures that are very similar. Words and phrases may be different from anything that we have heard before, but we sense that we are listening to a language, not just a jumble of sounds. A child very quickly identifies that structure and starts to communicate, even though its vocabulary may be very limited.

It was also noted that competence in using a language is not the same thing as intelligence (as measured by IQ tests), it is something shared by all. A person may be highly articulate without being able to read or write.

Learning a second language is of course a very different matter. We learn the grammar from books and struggle to get it right. Often the person who has a good working vocabulary in a foreign language and who pronounces it well lacks the subtlety of phraseology and idiom that comes automatically to the untrained native speaker.

But is it possible to learn a new language if you do not already have natural language? How could a new language make sense, unless you already have what amounts to an innate knowledge of the principles by which words are put together?

Contrast the way in which a second language is learned with that of the child who is developing his or her natural language. The rules of the new language are explained with reference to the natural one and justified by the fact that the person already knows that natural one. But how is that one justified? One would need to suggest some sort of pre-language, a body of innate rules for understanding what these strings of words signify. But how would you know that those rules are correct, except by suggesting an even more basic... and so on. This leads to an infinite regress. In order to justify *any* linguistic form, one needs to have some already accepted criterion by which to do so. The conclusion to this would seem to be that, for any language to make sense, there must be some innate linguistic starting point, itself needing no further justification.

## Wittgenstein

It is almost impossible to say anything about language without at some point mentioning Wittgenstein (1889–1951). In his early work, *Tractatus*, he was concerned with the validation of language, particularly as it related to the criteria used by science – in other words, he wanted to show the logic and evidence that lay behind statements. In particular, his approach was one in which language had a 'picturing' function, with its truth or falsity depending on whether or not it corresponded to things and events in the world. In this, he places the self outside the world:

> The subject does not belong to the world, but is a limit of the world.

This is most important, for any attempt to describe the self is going to fail, if that language is required (in order to be meaningful) to 'correspond' to some physical state of affairs.

---

**IN OTHER WORDS**

Whatever we describe, it cannot be the subject self, for as soon as we describe it, we externalise it and make it part of 'our' world, standing out over there against us. The self cannot describe itself, unless it tries to make itself an object. And if it tries to do that, it loses the very essence of its selfhood.

---

His later work on language was more concerned with the various functions performed by language. Meanings were given in terms of function, rather than in terms of correspondence with external reality; something could be said to make sense in terms of the part it played within a particular way of speaking, rather than simply by pointing to something in the physical world.

Following this line of thought, one can therefore see the sense in understanding language about the mind and consciousness primarily in the context of what such language does. You describe feelings, for example, in order to communicate your hopes or wants to other people. You are not trying to give some alternative description of brain activity to a passing neuroscientist! The meaning of your thoughts and consciousness is therefore appreciated only within an appropriate context.

---

**KEY POINTS**

The structure of language, whether it is innate or socially defined, reflects the structure of thought. As we think, we speak to ourselves, we puzzle out issues, hold inner dialogues and weigh concepts. Language is a medium of communication simply because people share a common structure of thought – a structure which expresses itself through language, but is also shaped by language.

Language is public. A private language makes no sense, since concepts are conventional and reflect communication. Otherwise, why should certain sounds take on meaning?

If it were not for language, we would know only what we could experience for ourselves. Our past would be limited to our own memory and our world would be limited to our visible horizon. In a real sense, although we would be conscious, able to respond to stimuli, we would not be able to think in anything like the way we take for granted. We would look and see, but not be able to frame concepts to explain (to ourselves or others) *what* we see. Communal action would be based on signs and common intuition and therefore limited to the most primitive of need satisfaction.

In short, the philosophy of mind is really a study of that which is expressed through language and that which is largely generated by language. The mind is consciousness, memory and language. But consciousness and memory without language are no more than visual images, feelings and instinctive responses. Reflective consciousness, which is a distinctively human trait, requires language.

---

# Neuroscience

A key problem for cognitive science is how the brain manages to represent the world. In other words, how states in the brain actually 'appear' to us as colour, shapes, sounds and so on. How is it that we can use language, remember things, generate ideas? What is actually going on between our ears when this 'mental' activity is happening?

Traditionally, philosophers have used the mind to understand how the mind works. In other words, they have reflected on their experience and tried to extract from it some *a priori* principles. We shall look at this process again in Chapter 4.

What is radically different with today's cognitive science is that it has a quite different way of looking at what is happening. Neurobiology examines the brain and nervous system. It looks at the way in which neurones take information from other neurones at their dendritic synapses, process it and then send it out, through their axonal synapses, to other neurones. In other words – it looks at the biological systems in which mental activity is realised.

There is a key question to be explored here: How relevant is this examination of brain activity to an understanding of mind? Dualists would hold that the brain and the mind are very different – and that mental events are a different substance from brain states or (at the very least) that they are very different ways of describing the same phenomenon.

So you have two different sciences here: psychology deals with the mind and neurobiology deals with the brain and nervous system. Is it possible that, as neuroscience develops, these two disciplines will come together to give an explanation of the brain/mind phenomenon as a whole?

Of course, the question of *reductionism* would need to be examined here. If we say that neuroscience can actually tell us about the mind, are we claiming that the mind is reduced to or 'nothing but' brain states? Materialists would hold that there is no other mental substance and that mind is not to be found anywhere other than in those brain states – but they would then go on to say that 'mind' language deals with a level of complexity that is quite different from an examination of the firing rates of individual neurones in the brain. When one particular faculty is impaired through brain damage, other parts of the brain step in and try to cover the work that the damaged part had previously done. Hence the gradual recovery of mobility or speech for stroke victims, for example. Where the dedicated section of brain is no longer available, others step in.

Now, that suggests that the whole reason for the way in which the brain selects and handles work is based on a problem-solving paradigm, for if one part cannot solve a problem another part steps in and tries to do it instead.

### Example

Paul Churchland has argued (in Cummins and Cummins, see Further reading) that, with $10^{11}$ neurones and $10^3$ connections on each, you have a total of $10^{14}$ synaptic connections between cells and for each of those connections there can be perhaps ten different values – in terms of the 'weight' of response. This gives a vast array of responses to stimuli, which may be varied in response to feedback, positive or negative. In other words, by adjusting the weights of the millions of synaptic connections, the brain is able to 'learn' how to deal with situations; it does not need to be programmed with crude external data.

The sort of process that goes on in the brain is one that responds to many stimuli and it is extremely adaptable. This illustrates the way in which the brain may be able to develop through numerous small changes – exactly the sort of process seen generally in evolution.

In other words, neural networks 'learn' and can therefore respond to challenges from the environment.

Another relevant feature here is the biological and evolutionary development of the brain and nervous system. Darwin's theory of natural selection has shown that species as a whole develop characteristics because individuals possessing those characteristics have a tendency to survive and breed. Why then has humankind developed such a large brain, compared with other species?

Clearly, the answer lies in the functions that the brain and nervous system perform. Remembering things, communicating with others, solving puzzles, thinking how best to trap an animal or find other forms of food. All these things are mental — the more developed the mind, the more capable an animal might be of working out how to survive and particularly how to compensate for lack of strength and so on.

Hence the brain and nervous system would have developed simply because these gave individuals the ability to survive. In other words – they *solved problems*. Hence, although we may not know *how* the brain succeeds in representing complex phenomena, we know *why* it does so.

As neuroscience develops, we will learn more about the precise way in which parts of the brain function, about the patterning of neural activity and about how these correlate with what is experienced.

What neuroscience has done is to make a crude 'substance' dualism untenable. It is quite unrealistic, in considering how the biological system has developed, to claim that the mind is utterly separate from the body. Neither can it be a simple 'epiphenomenon' — any creature that has its mental representations as no more than a by-product of brain activity cannot survive for long in the jungle, for representations have a very practical function, to assess and respond to what is 'out there' in the world. But that takes us to an area we must explore a little further – evolutionary psychology.

# Evolutionary psychology

Is it possible to find a point in the history of life on this planet when 'mind' or 'consciousness' emerged? Is it possible to look back at very simple organisms and trace the moment when they can be said to be sentient, in other words, to be aware of their environment and to respond to it?

Clearly, different species of animals have different minds, with different abilities and levels of thought. What are the features of the development of *Homo Sapiens* that has led to our present mental abilities?

These questions, looking at the function of mind in different species, give an interesting slant on the human mind and particularly on its social nature. These things are explored by, for example, Daniel Dennett in *Kinds of Minds* (1996), and *Darwin's Dangerous Idea* (1995).

What we need to accept is that different species behave in very different ways and that it is dangerous to project onto one the thoughts of another. For example, ants work within a community, selflessly carrying out their respective roles. But are they thinking about such things – do they feel a responsibility to carry refuse away from the nest, for example? Or are they operating in mechanical and programmed ways, with none of the subtlety of the mental operations of more advanced species (advanced, that is, from a human perspective)? And how could we know whether an ant is thinking about what it is doing or simply getting on and doing it, mindlessly? If we knew why consciousness and mind has developed differently in different species, it might give us valuable insights into what mind actually *is*.

Evolution has become a scientific paradigm, through which many theories may be assessed. It is natural therefore to ask whether the theory of evolution might have something to contribute to our knowledge of the mind. One way of looking at the mind, which follows largely from the 'functionalist' approach, is to see it as a tool for problem solving. If humankind were presented with no challenges, it would not have developed tools and other things that have given it a leading edge in the evolutionary struggle.

Of course, the one thing that has given humankind the most important evolutionary advantage has been the development of language. With language, knowledge can be passed on from one generation to the next and therefore accumulates quickly. Without language, everything has to be learned from scratch with each new generation and that is a great limitation.

Evolution depends on success in coping with the environment – those who gain an advantage by having a particular quality breed and therefore increase the number of members of their species with that quality in the future. The brain is a key feature to be considered when examining the development of the higher apes and up to

repeated

**Example**

Let us consider, therefore, a simple mental ability that could give evolutionary advantage, the recognition of individual features or kinship recognition:

■ If it were impossible to recognise individuals, then everyone might be a friend or an enemy, a threat or a source of help. In a situation of some danger, it is therefore essential to be able to recognise those who belong to your own tribe or family in order to be able to combine resources in the struggle for existence.

■ Hence, the ability to recognise kinship is an important step towards banding together in kinship groups for mutual protection.

■ The one who remains a 'loner' becomes vulnerable.

■ The ability to co-operate with others will increase success in hunting and killing larger animals that might threaten a lone hunter.

■ Hence the mental ability to see, recognise and remember the appearance of kin gives an evolutionary advantage – hence it is a mental ability that will increase over time.

Evolution depends on success in coping with the environment – those who gain an advantage by having a particular quality breed and therefore increase the number of members of their species with that quality in the future. The brain is a key feature to be considered when examining the development of the higher apes and up to *Homo Sapiens*; there has been a significant increase in brain capacity as evolution towards humankind has progressed.

But the mechanism for developing the brain is the success that mental activity gives for survival in a competitive environment. Those who are able to devise tools to plan out strategies in co-operation with others are at an advantage. Larger brains make these functions possible. As we evolve as individuals, we go through a similar process of mental development. We are born with far more neural connections than we will ever use and we gradually – as we encounter the world and discover what we can do in it – build up

**COMMENT**

This approach implies a functionalist account of the mind. Consciousness is not identified with grey matter, but is expressed through the patterns and operations that go on within it.

And fundamentally, it is no more crazy to say that the mind is expressed through such patterns as it would be to say that a Mozart symphony is expressed through the various blowing and scrapings carried out by members of the orchestra. Physical expression is not the same thing as reductionism. Just as we do not have to ask where the symphony can be found, once all the instruments are playing, so we do not have to locate mind, once we are aware of the neural patterns that are operating in the brain. This, of course, is exactly what Ryle was talking about (see page 38). The key difference is that he concluded that mental operations were 'nothing but' the various bits and pieces of which they were comprised, thereby demolishing Descartes' idea of a separate mental *substance*, but tripping himself up by thinking that this means the mind was no more than a verbal usage – a convenient way of summing up physical activity. The whole study of consciousness today suggests that we do not have to accept Ryle's limited options – something can be real and expressed through the physical, without being either a linguistic form or an occult substance. And one of the ways in which we can think about those alternative non-physical modes of being real may be suggested by considering artificial intelligence, which we shall examine later.

patterns of brain activity, corresponding to our growing consciousness of the world.

In other words, the brain is the physical organ through which we lay down our experiences as memories and are thus able to learn, communicate and think.

Dennett sees the mind as made up of many devices that have a long evolutionary history. From the crude intentionality of simple creatures, to the mind of human beings, there is a development – through natural selection – in the direction of increased awareness of and sophisticated response to the environment.

He also points out how difficult it is to say at what point we can talk about creatures becoming conscious in the way that human beings are aware of their own consciousness. One of the key tests is an understanding of the experience of pain – and this has considerable moral significance, since creatures that are deemed to have awareness of pain are generally required to be treated in a way that reflects their suffering. Thus, for example, in any painful experiments they should be given an anaesthetic. The problem always comes in that grey area where it is not clear what is being experienced – does the ant or the earthworm experience pain?

But setting aside for the moment the point at which consciousness is detected, it is important to recognise, through considering the way in which evolution works, that what is important is not so much what the mind *is*, or where it is located even, but what it *does*. In other words, the mind is to be examined in terms of its function and, indeed, the same functions (e.g. taking action to avoid being eaten when confronted with a predator) can take many different forms in different creatures with different brain and nervous system configurations. So perhaps it would be far more useful to consider minds by examining the way in which they function, rather than the particular type of brain they use for that functioning. And this leads us in the direction of *functionalism*, a theory which has been particularly important in cognitive science because of its relevance to questions of artificial intelligence – for if a mind is a matter of doing rather than being, we might consider trying to get a computer to do it.

# Functionalism

Functionalism was a theory developed in the 1960s, particularly by Hilary Putnam (b. 1926), which became very influential in cognitive science. It has had its critics, of course, notably John Searle, whose key criticism of functionalism and artificial intelligence we shall examine in the next section.

Functionalism allows that mental states are real; they are seen as the causes of our responses to that which impinges on us. Not every response can be measured in terms of movement or language. For example, faced with a lion in the jungle, it might be a good policy to freeze, hoping that the lion will take no notice. Certainly, running away in such circumstances would be no use at all. Hence, the mental response to the fear is to do nothing. At one level, this cannot be observed or measured. Of course, there is always the possibility that a heart monitor can register fear even if not a single muscle is moved in flight. A behaviourist would take that as evidence for the mental state. Functionalism looks at the nature of the stimulus and the response that we make to it – and sees the primary function of the mind as sorting out how to respond to each given stimulus (just like a computer processing input data).

A problem for a materialist view of the mind is that it needs to examine the physical basis of mental activity and yet different forms of brain or computer, which may perform the same types of function, are very different from one another. Also, there is no way of showing how it is that a certain sequence of brain activity actually causes particular thoughts or sensations – and so, until we have a complete neurobiological mapping of the brain, it seems that the materialist is stuck.

From a functionalist point of view, however, there is no need to wait for a full analysis of the physical realisation before sorting out the function of a particular mental quality. Pain, for example, causes a physical reaction of curling up or flinching, as a result of the damage to tissue. Exactly how that is turned into the experience we call pain can be left to one side. Thus functionalists produce what amounts to a function map of the mind – showing the various operations it performs – but that map does not have to correlate precisely with the firing of neurones in the brain.

---

**COMMENT**

Functionalism is less concerned with the physical makeup of brains and more with the complexity of the way in which that physical makeup operates, and the way in which it is organised. The mental is seen not in what the physical *is*, but in what it *does*.

## Getting round the 'gap'

Functionalism is one way to get around Leibniz' gap (see page 21) by which there is always a gap between our description of a thought or cognition and our description of the mechanical process in our sensory organs or in our brain which corresponds to it. In other words, the problem of not being able to describe thought in physical terms.

Functionalism allows something to be described in terms of what it does, without having to specify exactly how it does it, or what physical form it takes.

### Example

A bottle opener can take many forms. You can have the basic corkscrew with a simply handle for pulling upwards. There are more elaborate versions that have side levers to pull the cork or those that pull it from the side. Some corkscrews simply require the user to keep turning in the same direction: once the screw is fully within the cork, the same movement extracts it from the bottle. At one time it was popular to have a hollow needle with a pump on the end, extracting the cork through compressed air. And, of course, within the world of bottles there are some that have caps rather than corks. These can be prised off with a variety of openers. Some bottle tops can simply be unscrewed by hand – so perhaps the human hand can also be classified as a bottle opener!

Clearly, there is no single description of a bottle opener. The only thing these things have in common is their function.

It is therefore realistic to expect that we should be able to speak of a mental function without having to describe the mechanics through which it works. On a functionalist basis, a computer that performs an operation, which in a human being would be described as the result of thinking, is actually 'thinking'. But that does not in any way mean that the function is carried out in the same way and using the same mechanism in the computer and in the human brain.

Now, functionalism relates interestingly to ideas of artificial intelligence. Even if pain is real, pain is not exactly the same thing as the firing of neurones that takes place while the damage is being sustained and the resulting flinch is taking place. Rather, the brain activity and the subsequent bodily movements are the vehicle through which the pain is realised. If this is so, then it is possible that the same mental reality can be realised in more than one material situation. So the same thing could be realised in a human brain and attached body, but also in a computer. If pain is not identified with neurones firing, then there is no difference in principle between neurones firing and the sequence of electronic relays tripping within a computer memory – different physical forms, expressing the same mental function.

But most functionalists are content to say that mental functions are realised in the physical processes in the brain or the computer memory, there is no 'other' separate material basis for mind. The sort of causes of things that we call mental are realised in those ordinary physical circuits or structures.

In a sense, this sounds rather materialist, without actually be behaviourist. The mental state is not the same as the behaviour (that would be behaviourist) but the mental state is the direct cause of the behaviour and that cause is physically located in the brain or the computer memory. Mental operations are therefore made up of the actions of physical components. However, whereas the individual physical actions are simple (the firing of neurones), they work together in complex patterns, which (rather like computer programmes) produce results that have meaning on an entirely different scale. You don't have to ask, while playing a computer game, about the status of individual bits of memory. Yet that game is actually composed of millions upon millions of such bits working together in sequence. In the same way, you do not understand a mental function simply by examining the physical structure within which it is realised.

**Structures and physical states**

One of the problems with functionalism is to see how a form of organisation, like the software programme on a computer, can actually *do* anything physical. On the one hand, it solves some problems, because if an experience can be realised in different physical structures (a human brain and an animal brain, for example), then we can say that a feeling or expression can be the same thing in different species. When an animal is in pain, I know what that is like, because I have the same structures, performing the same 'pain' function.

On the other hand, there is a difficulty here. If we are dealing with forms of organisation or structure, expressed through different physical forms, then how can that structure actually enter the physical causal chain? Surely what actually gets things done is the physical matter in the brain – the actual neurotransmitters and so on.

Hence there is a tendency for a functionalist account to fall back on what amounts to materialism, if the mental states it expresses are not (as in epiphenomenalism – see page 22) simply the impotent by-product of a physical system.

# Artificial intelligence

The idea of artificial intelligence becomes possible once thought is seen as a matter of computing – sorting out bits of information fed into the system by the senses. This is not a new idea; in fact it was put forward by Thomas Hobbes (1588–1679), who claimed that 'Reasoning is but reckoning' (*Leviathan*, 1651). Once you have the notion that thought is a matter of sorting through data, many of the problems associated with the dualist view of minds and bodies no longer apply. Thought is not occult or unknowable, but an operation performed on information provided by the senses. Hobbes saw mental activity as but the working of a material process, but the implications of that approach have been appreciated only during the latter part of the 20th century with the advent of computers which, by mechanical means, are able to perform actions which resemble what a human being does when he or she 'thinks'. The issue of whether that physical process can simply be identified with thought and consciousness will be considered later, as it is absolutely crucial for the whole of the philosophy of mind.

---

**COMMENT**

In the 17th century you have the great divide between Descartes (and the whole continental rationalist and idealist tradition that stemmed from his work) on the one hand and the English empirical tradition on the other, typified by Locke and Hume. Hobbes, a forerunner of that latter tradition, saw our perceptions as nothing but the effect of external stimuli on our sense organs and that all we can know comes to us through such perceptions. That fitted well with that empirical tradition, and – of course – fitted with the view Locke was to argue, that the mind is a *tabula rasa*, a blank sheet waiting to be filled with information from the senses.

Curiously, almost all the discussions of the mind/body problem – and the problem itself, come to that – have been based on the Cartesian approach. How different things might have been if the debate had stemmed from Hobbes.

---

A crucial further step needed to be taken before artificial intelligence could be created. It came in the form of the theory of logic, developed by George Boole (1815–1864). He saw thinking and logic as a matter of symbol manipulation and also that any complex argument or process could be broken down into its constituent parts. Complex truths were in theory reducible in this way to binary truth values – everything, in the last analysis, was a matter of yes/no or off/on. Clearly, the implication of this is that complex concepts and arguments can be built up by the addition of very large numbers of basic binary choices.

A computer is a machine that operates a formal system of logical operations. It manipulates data according to a set of instructions. Basically, it has an input device to feed data, a processor that determines what shall be done with each incoming piece of information and suitable output devices, depending on what the computer is required to do.

---

**The same mechanics**

If you find it difficult to equate the artificial process that goes on in a computer memory with the working of the mind, consider the material basis of both. The computer works on a binary sequence, comprising a huge number of individual 'off/on' switches, which in turn switch others off or on. Individually, their significance is not apparent, but cumulatively they form the computer programme and data, revealing and processing information at a level very far removed from the basic switches.

The human brain has a very similar structure. Individual neurones either fire or do not fire (in other words, they form the same 'off/on' pattern) and in turn cause many others either to fire or not fire. The patterns of neurone firing within areas of the brain are therefore not unlike patters of binary switching within the computer memory.

---

The fundamental question here is 'Can computers think?'. This was raised by Alan Turing (1912–1954), who did much important developmental work on computing. His approach was to set a computer a basic task, namely that it should be able to respond to questions in such a way that a person would not be able to know whether those answers were coming from a computer or another person, in other words, that it responded intelligently.

Naturally enough, in order for this to work, it was necessary to programme the computer in such a way that appropriate answers would be formulated in response to questions. This became known generally as the 'Turing Test' and it raises a whole range of questions, not just about AI, but about the nature of human cognition and the relationship between 'mind' and 'brain'.

The approach taken by Putnam and others could therefore be described as materialist but not reductionist or behaviourist. Mental operations are going on (they are not simply covert ways of describing bodily actions, as behaviourists claim) but they are not

---

**COMMENT**

We shall see later (page 77) that this view is attacked by John Searle in his well-known Chinese Room thought experiment. His argument is that, with suitable programming instructions, it would be possible for correct answers to be given to questions, without the person giving those answers (in Searle's case, marks on pieces of paper that turn out to be Chinese pictograms) actually understanding anything other than the application of the programmed rules. In other words, with programming, one could be fooled in ascribing artificial intelligence to a machine that was simply working through a set of rules.

---

separate from the material world. They are operations that are going on in the brain.

Thus, for example, if you have a human being and a computer playing chess, both are performing the same functions. Both are following a set of rules about how moves are to be made. The basic difference between them is that the human brain has many *other* sets of rules that it could be following, for all the other aspects of its life. But in the actual game being played out, it is not fundamentally different from the computer.

From the point of view of artificial intelligence, the problem is therefore reversed. It is not a matter of asking how a computer can have a 'mind', but of why we need to think of the human as having a 'mind' over and above the various operations that it performs through the functioning of the brain. Are we not, in that sense, computers – with our various input and output devices in the form of the senses and creative activities, and the firing of neurones in our central processor unit between our ears being the means by which we relate the one to the other?

Of course, one crucial difference between the responses of a computer and a human being is that the inputs and outputs of the human being have meaning or significance; they are not impersonal. The human being has a reason for doing what he or she does. In other words, human thought is a semantic formal system (a process that operates logically, and which also expresses meaning).

**COMMENT**

Functionalism encouraged the study of AI simply because, for functionalists, mental operations were an activity that could be expressed in a number of different physical contexts, much the same way as a computer programme could be run on a variety of different hardware. But, if the phenomena of consciousness were related to function rather than to the physical makeup of brains, there seemed no reason why the same aspect of consciousness should not operate on a very different kind of 'brain', namely a computer.

For functionalism, mental activity is a form of software, not part of the hardware that is running it. One could therefore examine mental functioning without having to have detailed information about the brain and its method of operation.

What then is the essential difference between the human being and the computer? Some possibilities were clearly set out by John Haugeland in his book *Semantic Engines: An Introduction to Mind Design* (MIT Press, 1981). He suggests that those who claim that computers are essentially different from humans take one of two general lines of argument:

1 **The 'hollow shell' argument**. This suggests that semantic engines (i.e. computers that appear to use meaningful symbols) are not intelligent, but merely act 'as if' they are. They are a fake or a 'hollow shell' because they lack a special something that is required for real thought.

   That 'special something' could be:
   - Consciousness – although it is very difficult to specify what consciousness is.
   - Original intentionality – in other words, the computer is programmed, but the human acts for his or her own reasons
   - Caring – the computer does not have any concern about what is being processed, whereas the human being is committed and concerned about the things

thought about and can have very powerful emotional reactions to them.

2 **The 'poor substitute' argument.** This suggests that computers are good at doing a limited range of tasks, but that they will never become powerful enough to be able to get near what we know of human intelligence or have anything like the range of abilities that we associate with common sense.

---

**COMMENT**

■ None of the arguments against AI reaching the human level is absolute. Since Haugeland's book was written, for example, computer power has increased enormously. Children now play with computers many times more sophisticated than anything available in the 1980s. Might that process continue indefinitely? If so, can the 'poor substitute' argument hold?

■ Notice also that consciousness, intentionality, emotional involvement and commitment are all very difficult to define, but may actually be programmable. Indeed, education and society aims at increasing social and emotional awareness. Is that not a case of programming for intentionality and emotional involvement? If so, apart from the quantity of computing power available within the human brain and the range and scope of the input stimuli from birth onwards which informs the growth of the intelligence and consciousness, what is the difference between human and computer?

■ The whole process of child development, as explored within psychology, to say nothing of the problems of psychopathology, show ways in which thought and feeling later in life may be influenced by childhood experiences. The youthful computer is programmed (or rather, programmes itself – a

> point we shall look at later in terms of neural
> networks) at a fearful rate. Sometimes it is
> programmed with ideas that are potentially harmful
> later in life.
> ■ If programming does not work, how do we account
> for the phenomena of hypnosis or most obviously NLP
> (neuro-linguistic programming)? Therapy assumes
> that a programme may be examined and improved,
> changing the way in which the 'personality' responds
> to stimuli.

## Functionalism and AI

From a functionalist viewpoint, consciousness and intelligence is a matter of the patterns and structures that are formed by complex physical processes, such as can go on in a brain or a computer memory. One thinker who has been particularly influential in presenting mental processes as being computational and formal is Jerry Fodor (b.1935).

In general, the functionalist approach sees mental operations as being like the software that is running on the computer, while the brain itself is the hardware. This enables a clear distinction to be made between the formal operations (following the commands of the programme), the semantic content (information that is being processed) and the material base that is supporting this function (the brain or computer memory).

The functionalist is thus able to see the same mental phenomena in different 'hardware' – and hence that it is possible to use the computer model for an understanding of consciousness and also to be able to say that, at a certain level, a computer actually has a mind and has a consciousness that is not essentially different in character (although on a very different scale in terms of complexity) from human consciousness.

Now the computer analogy is particularly useful in this debate. A computer programme is not part of the hardware, but it does not exist except as embodied in the hardware. Also, the work of the computer is carried out as a result of actual electrical impulses in the memory, but that does not exclude the programme from being the cause. To say that an action is carried out either by the memory or by the programme is just an example of what Ryle called the 'category mistake'. What is supplied to make the computer work is the logical set of rules that is expressed in what we call the 'programme'. But, of course, every instruction in that programme is there because a human programmer has chosen for it to work in that particular way.

---

**IN OTHER WORDS**

A human mind devises a programme for a computer and is then surprised that the programme works just like a human mind!

---

If the mind is not just a result of physical activity in the brain, but actually causes it (as the programme that is running causes particular sequences of activity within the computer memory), where does that mind 'come from'?

Clearly, there are some interesting possibilities here. Does it come from social conditioning? Here we get into issues of language and how concepts are learned. By some kind of genetic inheritance? This leads us to consider if there are any innate ideas, rather than ideas that come to us as a result of what is conveyed by the senses.

---

**COMMENT**

Artificial intelligence does not, it seems to me, contribute a great deal to the issue of understanding the nature of human consciousness. If we could construct a human being with a brain and sensory system, with the ability to express itself as humans do, then it would be indistinguishable from a human being – and we would be no further forward. We would be no more able to examine the nature of its consciousness than we are that of any human being now (see the comment under Zombies, page 111).

All it could show is that there is no *separate mental substance*. But (sorry, Descartes) most of us knew that already!

We have here yet another example of an issue that bedevils the philosophy of science. Analysis does not, in itself, show the nature and operation of complex entities. In other words, you cannot understand the nature of a motoring holiday by a careful analysis of the various bits and pieces that go to make up a motorcar engine. We cannot claim (as some of those engaged in AI appear to) that one day, when we have an absolutely 100 per cent knowledge of every bit of that car, such that we can build an identical model from scratch, we will then have a complete sense of what the motoring holiday is about. The perfectly understood and reproduced car will tell us no more about that than does the present one.

## AI and neural computing

So far we have considered artificial intelligence in terms of computers that are programmed to receive and respond to stimuli. The mind is then seen functionally; in terms of the calculations about how we should respond to the stimuli we receive.

But is that how human beings actually operate? Clearly, it is not. There is no point at which a young brain is programmed – it learns things gradually as it goes along. It has many influences and sorts out values and principles from them, but that is something that each individual does for himself or herself – no two people have exactly the same mind, since no two people have had the same experiences that have shaped their thinking.

Neural computing is rather different; it is the term used for building computers that can learn for themselves, rather than being programmed. In this, it is the conscious attempt to get a physical device to 'grow' a mind, in the same way as a human being.

The difference between these two forms of computing illustrates a feature of Ryle's argument in *The Concept of Mind*. Ryle distinguished between 'knowing that' and 'knowing how'. The former is the information that you have been fed by the senses; the latter is the awareness of how to perform some action. AI tends to concentrate on getting computers to 'know that' and to come up with the appropriate responses as a result. Neural computing tries to produce computers that will 'know how'.

He speaks of the 'intellectualist legend', which is the idea that when someone wants to perform an intelligent task, he or she first of all has to think of all the rules involved and then apply them. That, of course, is exactly what a computer does, since all the rules have been ready programmed into its memory. Rather, Ryle argues that intelligent action is a matter of instinctively knowing what one wishes to do in a situation, irrespective of any rules.

## Example

An artist or composer who merely followed the rules would never produce anything truly original. Their work would be branded 'derivative'. A key feature of human intelligence and creativity is that it can see possibilities within a situation or ways of handling new experiences, which are utterly original.

Neural networks offer the possibility that, one day, computers might be able to learn from new situations and might therefore become creative. Every time something happens to a human being, that experience goes into his or her memory and will contribute to future decisions. 'I won't do that again!' or 'I'd like some more of that!' is the key to learning.

If minds were programmed, we would all end up with a common set of values and assumptions about life. As it is, the ever-present possibility of becoming warped, damaged or inspired by life ensures that we remain remarkably different.

How exactly neural networking in the computer world might simulate the process of human learning is a technical matter and the production of machines that can learn with anything like the sophistication of the human mind is far in the future, if indeed it ever becomes possible. For our purposes, however, it does highlight a major problem with conventional AI and points out the engaged and ever-learning features of human minds.

In *The Emperor's New Mind* (1989) Professor Roger Penrose of Oxford argued that it would be impossible to create an intelligent robot because consciousness required self-awareness and that was something a computer could not simulate. It was a very serious attack on some of the rather naive and optimistic claims of those working in the field of artificial intelligence, but it does not really address the possibility of a computer which can learn, develop its own personal history and thus create its own form of individual self-awareness.

---

**COMMENT**

A crucial area for exploration in considering the nature of the human mind – or rather the way in which humans operate mentally – is to consider the process of education. From the moment of birth, a child is taking in information and learning. Day by day a gradual pattern emerges that allows the growing infant to cope with its world. At no stage is it formally 'programmed' with a ready-made adult mind. The mind has 'grown' as this very complex being, with its brain, nervous system and general biochemistry, and has encountered and responded to the world.

If this were not so, why do babies respond so well to positive stimulus? Why are problems later in life related to childhood traumas? Why do depression and elation, as ways of seeing the world, relate to the experiences we have? Why do people change their views as they get older? Why do the minds of those with degenerative disease become so diminished? Why do drugs alter a person's mood or perception?

It is really inconceivable that the mind could be other than intimately related to the whole organism. To attempt to separate it off, making it a detached, non-extended substance, makes nonsense of everything from the desire to relax over a social drink, to the 'high' that comes from a good exercise session.

We are not minds loosely attached to bodies, we are thinking and feeling beings. Of all the areas in the philosophy of mind that illustrate this, the debate over AI perhaps makes it clearest, for the attempt to 'import' a mind and load it onto a machine is no more than a caricature of a truly thinking and feeling being.

---

## The infinite background problem

An additional problem here is raised by a philosopher who has nothing whatever to do with artificial intelligence – Martin Heidegger (1889–1976). He was an existentialist philosopher, concerned with the way in which people choose what to do, understand themselves and live in an authentic way. One feature of his thinking about this was the fact that people are, to use his term, 'thrown' into their particular life – most of the circumstances we have to deal with are already given and not of our own choosing. In order to understand any choice, therefore, one needs to know something of the circumstances in which it is being made. But those circumstances are determined by yet other factors and those by others still. Equally, the way we respond to situations is influenced by our own personal history, since memory plays a vital role in choosing how we are to act.

The problem, therefore, is that there is a theoretically infinite background of facts that would need to be taken into account in order to fully understand even the most straightforward of choices.

This tends to complicate the functionalist argument – since it is not simply a matter of processing particular input data and coming up with a response. The mind is something that takes into each decision its own history and, where it is responding to language, we need also to be aware that the person speaking or writing also has his or her own infinite background and so on.

Thus the image of the mind as a basic machine with information being fed into it in a linear way and a succession of outputs at the other is very limited. In reality there is a complex network of meanings, values and significances – a network that stretches out in all directions which we can never fully appreciate.

# The Chinese Room

One of the most important considerations of the scope of AI and a critique of the assumption that a computer programme is in some way the equivalent of a mind was put forward in 1980 by the American philosopher, John Searle. He set out to consider whether or not it was correct to say that a computer could actually understand (as opposed to manipulate) information, taking as his starting point the usual description of a computer as a 'formal symbol manipulation system'. In other words, the computer is programmed with a range of symbols and rules and it follows these in order to produce its output.

He distinguished first of all between a 'weak' view of AI, which simply claims that AI is of value for helping us understand the way in which the mind works and a 'strong' view, that a computer programme is in fact a 'mind' and that it has cognitive states. It is this 'strong' view that Searle sets out to challenge.

He does so by considering our ability to understand stories. When a person is told a story in a language he or she knows, the person can understand that story and respond correctly when questions are asked. But if you don't know the language, you can't understand the story and are quite unable to respond to questions.

Now, Searle considers the situation of a person who knows absolutely no Chinese. He is locked in a room and given a batch of Chinese writing. None of the characters mean anything to him. Then he is given a second batch, along with a set of instructions in English. These instructions help him to relate the second batch of characters to the first one.

Now, the first set represents a story in Chinese, and the second a set of potential questions and answers about it. The English instructions effectively link one set to another, so that the person can match up one character with another without needing to understand anything of what they actually mean.

A set of questions in Chinese is then fed into the room. Following the instructions, the person inside matches up the appropriate Chinese characters and posts out the required answer. If the instructions are followed correctly, a Chinese speaker on the outside will be receiving answers which would suggest that the person inside the room is able to read Chinese, understand the story and respond appropriately. But, of course, he actually understands not a word.

Searle's argument is that exactly the same thing is happening in the computer, in the situation that, according to the Turing Test, would suggest that a computer is 'thinking'. The computer actually understands nothing.

Searle looks at the claims of AI and comes to the conclusions that, just as he can manipulate Chinese characters without understanding them, so a computer can manipulate a set of formal symbols without actually knowing anything at all of what they stand for. All the computer has done is regurgitate what the programmer has put into it, it has not actually known anything or been aware of the significance of its operation. In other words, it has not been 'thinking'.

Now this is a drastic challenge to AI. Searle is asking that those who suggest that 'strong' AI is possible (i.e. that you can create a computer which actually has a mind) that it should be possible to say exactly what distinguished mental from non-mental. If the answer is that a machine has a mind if its responses are intelligible, then his 'Chinese Room' argument proves that false – for the man in the room has no knowledge of Chinese, although appearing to respond intelligently.

Towards the end of the argument, Searle makes two important points that link AI to the theories of mind that we have been considering earlier:

■ That the traditional test of an 'intelligent response' for deciding if a computer can think is effectively both behaviourist and operationalist. In other words, it is decided only on what can be observed, not on any direct awareness of the process of thought.

■ That it assumes a dualism of programmes and hardware (with the programme seen as the 'mind' and the hardware upon which it runs as the 'brain') but that dualism separates the mind from its material matrix. True, it is not exactly the same dualism that was proposed by Descartes, but it certainly cuts out the possibility of a direct description of the mental in physical terms.

To the traditional question 'Can machines think?' his answer is 'Yes' – but only very special machines, namely human brains. He concludes:

> If mental operations consist in computational operations on formal symbols, then it follows that they have no interesting connection with the brain; the only connection would be that the brain just happens to be one of the indefinitely many types of machines capable of instantiating the program... AI has little to tell us about thinking, since it has nothing to tell us about machines. By its own definition, it is about programs, and programs are not machines. Whatever else intentionality is, it is a biological phenomenon, and it is as likely to be as causally dependent on the specific biochemistry of its origins as lactations, photosynthesis or any other biological phenomena.
>
> (*Minds, Brains and Programs*, in Cummins and Cummins, p.151)

In other words, the process of cognition and intentionality (in other words, acting with purpose) is a phenomenon of a whole organism. It is linked to what it means biologically to be a human being and therefore it cannot be equated with a programmed set of instructions in the brain.

But it remains a possibility for Searle that neuroscience might one day be able to give an account of the brain that would explain how consciousness is caused and that would (for him) finally overcome the mind/body problem.

A key feature of Searle's approach, brought out very clearly in his book *The Rediscovery of Mind* (1992), is that it was always a mistake to assume that something is either mental or physical, but that it cannot be both at the same time:

> The brain causes certain 'mental' phenomena, such as conscious mental states, and these conscious states are simply higher-level features of the brain.
>
> The fact that a feature is mental does not imply that it is not physical; the fact that a feature is physical does not imply that it is not mental.
>
> (op. cit. p. 14)

Searle is making a crucially important point here. If he is right, then much of what has been done in the philosophy of mind is simply mistaken, since it has been based on invalid assumptions.

Searle's position seems to be like that of 'property dualist', since his 'higher-level' description of a physical process is simply describing it in a different way (namely, an holistic way) from that of the reductive analyst, who is concerned only with the lower levels.

However, the difference between Searle's position and that of a 'property dualist' approach is that, for Searle, there is a single reality that is multi-layered and our language reflects that multi-layering. This is not quite the same as saying that a single reality may be described in two different ways, since it implies that the layering is a feature of reality, not just of language.

He therefore introduces 'concept dualism' (as an alternative to 'substance dualism' or 'property dualism'). A concept can refer to something physical or to something mental, but not to both. What he is concerned to maintain is the standard scientific way of looking at the material world, alongside the indisputable fact of consciousness:

> What I want to insist on, ceaselessly, is that one can accept the obvious facts of physics – for example, that the world is made up entirely of physical particles in fields of force – without at the same time denying the obvious facts about our own experiences – for example, that we are all conscious and that our conscious states have quite specific irreducible phenomenological properties.'
>
> (op. cit. p. 28)

---

**IN OTHER WORDS**

You don't have to choose between materialism and some form of dualism, whether as presented by the older debates or in the new context of cognitive science. You can – and should – have the best of both worlds.

---

# Intentionality

The psychologist Brentano (1838–1917) argued that all consciousness was directed towards something. Thus, we are not simply conscious, but also conscious 'of'. Ideas and beliefs are related to actions and may be judged by their value to us. This is a pragmatic approach and parallels work by William James (in *Psychology*, 1890).

In other words, we can describe things as conscious in that they have intentionality, in other words, if they are goal orientated and have purpose and aim in what they do. But, of course, at the simplest level, the creature concerned may not be able to reflect or comment on that purpose. Now, it is far from clear how one would understand the mind of a very simple creature, but Daniel Dennett, for example, sees the 'intentional stance' – the strategy of treating small living things as if they were governed by rational choices and goals, as a useful one.

### Example

A white blood cell has a particular purpose; it is part of the system of repair and management for the body. A white blood cell is definitely goal orientated. But should one say that it has a mind?

In modern discussion of consciousness, intentionality refers generally to the way in which our minds handle information 'about' something. I may think about an external object or use language that involves concepts that are shared with others. The mind is not just self-referential, it does not just happen to be in a particular state, it is intentionally orientated; it is dealing 'with' something. If conscious states did not refer to anything other than themselves, they would serve no purpose and would hold no interest for us. It is intentionality that gives the mind a task – that sets it to work on something. Thus, for example, all language is intentional.

As we look at something, our mind gives it attention and draws into its understanding of it a very complex set of awareness, based on our other experiences and enhanced by our memory.

Clearly, intentionality implies that the mind has conscious representations of external things. It handles informational states that represent external features of the world. But if we equate consciousness with information about external states, then there are

### Example

The concept of 'a bowl of fruit' is actually quite a complex one. It involves the understanding that fruit is good to eat, that one might have it available at home, that it could be out on display, because it is the sort of food that one might have between meals, and so on. One might recall various artists who have painted bowls of fruit. One may remember the occasion on which one was given that particular bowl or the moment in the shop when the fruit was bought. A simply act of looking at an object may therefore be a complex mixture of memories and experiences, which the mind holds together in that single experience.

quite a few things, like simple measuring instruments, which hold such information without being conscious. Is a barometer 'conscious' of air pressure? Does the bar scanner 'know' that goods have been passed over it? Does the gearbox 'know' that you have selected reverse rather than drive?

There are many things that can influence what we see as having an 'intentional stance'. Thus Dennett, in *Kinds of Minds* (1996) points out that we may perhaps perceive minds only within certain parameters of size and speed of action. If something is very large or very slow, then it is difficult to see what is happening. Plants, for example, may turn to face the sun, in this they are *sensitive* to their environment and *respond* to it. This suggests that they have an intentional stance. If a person or animal swung round to get the benefit of light or turned languidly while sunbathing, one would assume – from the fact that the person was aware of the benefits of the sun and wanted to make use of them – that the action was a clear sign of consciousness. A plant may do exactly the same thing – but may do it very slowly. Competition, rivalry, the quest for extra nutrition and sunlight: the rat race life of plants is only displayed to us by means of speeded-up film. If they moved as quickly as animals, we would find it difficult not to think of them as conscious.

# A simple consciousness?

If consciousness relates to informational states, the logical conclusion is that consciousness exists across a very wide range of objects, both animate and inanimate. If this idea is unacceptable, it is possible to add another qualification – namely that, for consciousness, the information must have the effect of controlling behaviour. In other words, the barometer is not conscious, since it does nothing with the information that can be read from it. But what would we then say about a barometer with a robot attached, such that, every time the pressure dropped, the robot would collect an umbrella from a cupboard and set it near the door, in case of rain? Would such a barometric robot have consciousness?

Notice that such questions bring us back to the functionalist view of mind, and to the basics of much discussion of artificial intelligence – we are back on the input (representations), processing and output (controlled behaviour) way of examining consciousness.

## Crazy!

We all sense which things are conscious and which are not. We know that the mouse crouching in a corner, shuddering while the cat plays with it, is experiencing fear – although, to be fair, we cannot know exactly what it is like to be a frightened mouse. By way of contrast, the elaborate piece of robotic equipment that moves about a room avoiding furniture may look conscious and yet we automatically sense that there is no conscious life, just the obedience to programmed instructions.

The curious thing is that we all know these things and yet the functionalist definition of what it means to be conscious – processing information and responding to it – makes it actually very difficult not to come to the conclusion that some sort of primitive consciousness is found at almost every level of reality. Hence, we end up with the crazy notion of a thermometer being conscious of temperature. But is that any more bizarre than the robotic and mindless behaviour of people who are (theoretically) capable of conscious choice?

Clearly, for something to have a mind, it must have an intentional stance (being sensitive and responding to its environment), but it seems to need something else as well, something that a barometer, however sensitive, simply does not have. For Dennett, this is *sentience*, but it is not easily defined. A dictionary definition says simply that it is the quality of having the power of perception through the senses. But then one would need to define the way in which an ear, for example, is inherently different from the mechanism of a barometer or an eye from the photocells and image processing power of a digital camera.

## Active knowing...

In assessing the perspectives given by functionalism and intentionality, it is important to realise that the mind plays a very active role in cognition of any sort. We do not just experience 'anything', but a succession of 'somethings'. We sort them out and relate to them.

In comparing different kinds of minds and the way they work, Daniel Dennett points out that animals have evolved to consume information. The further up the evolutionary path it finds itself, the more each living thing needs to take an active role is assessing and responding to its environment. In evolutionary terms, if you can move only slowly, then you need good hearing and eyesight to detect and avoid predators. Survival depends on your information gathering and processing – and hence these are developed, as the relatively blind and deaf get eaten at a younger age and those aware of their environment survive to breed. Active knowing is the key to survival, to breeding and hence to the development of the species. A passive mind is of little use.

And, of course, the way the mind does all this active knowing leads us to ask how we can know anything at all, what is the process by which raw information is turned into a view of the world that can guide action. This is where the philosophy of mind starts to overlap with epistemology – the theory of knowledge – to which we will turn in the next chapter.

# 4 | MIND AND THE THEORY OF KNOWLEDGE

## To know is to remember

Plato held that one could have opinions about particular objects presented to the senses, but that certain knowledge was limited to the ideal realm of the 'forms', universals of which particular things were but pale copies. But clearly, the forms could not be seen directly. Plato therefore believed that all true knowledge was a matter of remembering; that the ideas of the forms are already innate in us and guide us to have our opinions about the particular things we see.

Now, we need not be concerned here about Plato's theory of knowledge itself, but it does have crucial implications for his view of the mind. If Plato is correct, then the mind has within itself a set of principles and general ideas that are there *before* any experience. We recognise things in the world as being, for example, a particular breed of dog or species of tree, because we already have some general knowledge of what we mean by 'dog' or 'tree'. The mind is certainly not the product of cumulative experience, built up by responding to the world, but comes to us, as it were, ready formed with a stock of eternal truths.

One standard criticism of Plato's theory runs like this:

- I know that this thing I see before me is a man.
- I do so because I already have a general concept 'man'.
- But, how do I know that this particular man is in fact a particular example of the general concept 'man', unless there is a 'third man' to whom they can both be related?
- Thus I can never be sure that this particular thing resembles the general 'form'.

This is a real problem for mind and the theory of knowledge. How can we show that our idea of something actually resembles what is out there to be experienced? I can not describe 'tree' without describing a particular tree. What then is this general concept that is not any tree in particular?

Few today might use the way we know things as an argument for reincarnation, as Plato did, but the issue of whether we have innate ideas is still very relevant. Clearly, we see things 'as', rather than just registering sense impressions. But such 'seeing as' implies that we have concepts and general principles by which we make sense of particular sensations. How have we acquired those concepts? Are we programmed with them – rather as Chomsky suggested that we were born with a natural facility to recognise and learn a language? Are they structural features of the brain? How can you have concepts without experiences? In other words, what could the general concept 'tree' mean for someone who had never seen a particular tree?

What is clear from Plato's approach is that the mere recording of sense data may be reported as a matter of opinion, but does not offer certainty. But what is certainty, anyway, in this context?

# Mind and certainty

Of what, then, can we be certain? This was the key question asked by Descartes – and his view of the separation of mind from body that came from it has been, as we have already seen, hugely influential.

In particular, how can we know that the perceptions we have actually resemble objects that are external to us? The philosopher Montaigne (1533–1592) argued that if one had never seen Socrates, one could not claim that a portrait of the philosopher was a good likeness. If we cannot know things except through our perceptions, how can we ever know whether or not those perceptions are accurate?

John Locke had argued that there is a basic resemblance between our perceptions and the external world. He had to do this, because he believed that the mind started off as a blank sheet of paper and only built up knowledge through experience. Locke saw the mind as fundamentally a storing and sorting facility – making sense of experiences. While he recognised that some aspects of experience (the secondary qualities of colour, taste etc.) were related to our sense organs, the primary qualities of extension and number were external to us and not mind dependent.

## Descartes' dilemma

Descartes was much influenced by the general scepticism of his day. He recognised the force of Montaigne's argument that one could not know whether perceptions gave a true picture of reality. He knew that in dreams he could experience what he believed to be real at the time, only to find on awakening that it had been no more than a dream. Asking the fundamental question 'By what criterion can you show that this is true?' he realised that certainty could only be given, if the basis on which one made that judgement was certain. But what if that basis were also open to question? You can't prove that something is true unless you have a criterion of which you are certain, but you can't prove *that* without something else being shown to be certain and so on. In the end, there seemed no fixed point of certainty – a sceptical view that was widespread in Descartes' day.

Against Plato's innate knowledge on the one hand, and Locke's knowledge through senses on the other, Descartes recognised the force of scepticism. He therefore needed to find that elusive point of certainty, without which all claims would remain vulnerable to the sceptic's challenge.

The vehicle he uses to express this (see *Mediation II*) is a powerful and malicious genius, which is determined to deceive him. Faced with such a deceiver, of what can he be certain? Of his body? Of his movements? He recognises that bodily movements can be experienced in dreams, when they are clearly not real, so he cannot be sure of any of them and therefore cannot trust his sensations. What then of thought; can he doubt that he is a thinking being? And, of course, unable to doubt that one thing (since the act of doubting was in itself an intellectual act) he arrived at '*I think therefore I am*'.

Hence his dualism – and all that has followed from it – is rooted in his theory of knowledge. It was the one means of countering the force of sceptical doubt. But the price of that certainty is that the mind (and self) is limited to its thinking function and is effectively removed from the world of the senses. Safely removed from the world that can be known and sceptically challenged, Descartes' mind cannot be doubted, *but can it do anything*?

---

**COMMENT**

Descartes presented the problem in terms of a demon deceiver, gradually showing that all he might have assumed to be true was in fact a deception. For him it was a 'thought experiment' – the testing out of a radical hypothesis. On account of this, he has often (and even at the time) been criticised for being a sceptic. This is somewhat unfair, although understandable. His 'demon deceiver' thought experiment aimed to expose the force of the sceptical argument, in order to find a point of certainty from which he could start to build up his theory of knowledge. His task was therefore a positive rather than a negative one. His judicious use of systematic doubt was designed to break down habitual notions and assumptions.

---

Notice for now that we cannot separate our understanding of what the mind is from the process by which we gain knowledge or justify our claims to knowledge. Do we pre-date our experiences, or are we a product of them? Is there some separate, eternal 'me' that has a reality independent of the circumstances in which I find myself or am I inevitably moulded and shaped by everything that happens, my initially blank mind learning and developing as it passes through life?

---

**COMMENT**

Although we'll return to these things later, notice the ethical and political implications of all this. If you are entirely moulded by your environment, then it (rather than you) is responsible for your actions. The poor rat in the Skinner box has been programmed to keep touching its lever in the hope of reward. If all we learn comes through our experience, are we any more independent of our circumstances than that rat?

> By the same token, is it ever possible to encounter someone whose mind touches on universal themes that seem in stark contrast to his or her environment – rising above circumstances, so to speak, to display something that cannot be accounted for sociologically?
>
> How we treat people will be coloured by the conclusions we reach on this question. Do I wish to be seen by you as someone who is simply a product of a certain upbringing and environment? Can my mind have ideas that are not given by that environment?

## Berkeley's approach

In Chapter 2 we outlined Berkeley's reasons for saying that all we can know are our sense perceptions and that, although we assume that they correspond to an external world, nevertheless we have no direct knowledge of such a world, only of our perception of it (see page 35).

Knowledge, therefore, for Berkeley, is limited to thinking about sense perception and the concepts by which we make sense of it. We cannot somehow get outside, or around, our perceptual apparatus to get an alternative view of the world, by which we can then assess its reliability. The object and our sensation of it are the same thing; our world is a world of ideas. Now, for Berkeley, one can think about and abstract from sensation, but one cannot get away from the basic feature of the mind as 'that which perceives'.

# We see it our way

What does it mean to perceive something? I see a creature in front of me and know that it is a cat – no problem. But actually, in order to see this thing as a cat there are a number of mental operations to be performed. To start with, size. The cat may be near or far, but – by the way in which my eyes focus and in comparison with other things of which I know the size – I calculate that the object is a certain size. But that is not simply something that comes with the impact of light rays on the retina of my eyes; it is a mental operation.

But what makes it a 'cat'? Not its colour – for there are cats of many different colours. What about having four legs and a tail? Fine, but I will have sympathy for the three-legged cat, and have no reason for claim that a Manx cat is not feline simply because it lacks a tail. The process of seeing a cat therefore involves a number of straight computational processes, but more particularly an appreciation of which features are essential for it to be called a 'cat' and which are incidental. My perceiving of a cat is therefore related to my education; I have been told (with many examples) that certain things are to be called 'cats' and so that is how I now categorise them.

Cats, of course, are an obvious example. Take the more subtle forms of the same dilemma. You taste the wine from a bottle whose label has been inconveniently covered. If you are a connoisseur of wines, you may immediately guess where it is from, its vintage, perhaps the particular vineyard. It is not that the novice has a different experience, but that – without training and the development of a suitable palate – wines cannot be experienced with such subtlety.

## No ordinary brandy

On a visit to Cognac, I was able to look through the glass panels of the doors into the tasting room. There the most experienced tasters, with racks of *eau de vie* in front of them, work to achieve exactly the right blend of flavours to produce their particular style of brandy. To learn exactly how to identify that taste takes many years. The nose of the head taster is a valuable possession and the next generation of nose is already in training to take over on the retirement of the present one!

Don't try telling anyone in that room that everyone has the same sensation when tasting brandy. They have trained for years to develop the art of taste!

What do we learn from this?

■ That the subtlety and complexity of an experience is related to the training and abilities of the person who does the experiencing.

> ■ To expect a simple computer to analyse with the
> subtlety of a human being is rather like putting a
> novice in among the expert tasters. It lacks suitable
> training.

## Innateness

Immanuel Kant (1724–1804) argued that the mind imposes categories (space, time and causality) upon experience and therefore that is has an active rather than passive role. The implication here is that there are certain concepts, for example causality, which are innate, in the sense that we are predisposed to think that everything will have a cause and that we have no option but to see everything falling within an overall framework of space and time.

But why do we appear to have these innate ideas or structures? Why does our mind have to work in that way? Plato believed that the self or soul was immortal and had lived many times before. Hence, he believed that people could know things by recollection – in other words, that (as far as this lifetime is concerned) they had innate knowledge. This is discussed in his dialogue *Meno*, where he asks a servant boy a series of mathematical questions and observes how he works out the answers. He concludes that the boy could not have been taught those answers in this life; therefore he must have recalled them from past lives. In practice, what he recognises is that there are basic logical abilities that appear innate – and his doctrine of recollection is his explanation of that phenomenon.

Descartes took a similar view (as explained in his *Optics*), namely that when the senses transmit information to the mind, that information is quite different from the experience that arises because of it. It becomes, as it were, the occasion for the mind to form its ideas, which is an innate faculty it has. And, of course, the reason Descartes holds this is that, according to his mechanics, the senses can only communicate through the physical movement of bodies – and he has no way of translating such physical movement into the objects of thought. Hence, the conceptions that form our basic awareness, as well as our more formal ideas, are innate. They may be triggered by the senses, but cannot be created by them.

Locke pointed out that the reason people argued for innate ideas was that there were certain things that were universally agreed and that such agreement suggested that everyone was born with them. He argued that you could not use universal agreement as an argument for innateness unless you could show that there was no other reason why all should agree. He points out that logical statements (e.g. something cannot both be and not be) may appear to be universal, but that in fact most people in the world have never thought about the matter at all, so they cannot be said to have assented to it. He also points out that children and idiots have no idea of what such things might mean – whereas, if such logical claims were indeed innate, then they would immediately recognise them to be true. Indeed, he sees the function of reason as the discovery of things not yet known on the basis of what is already known, but why should it do so if all knowledge is innate?

His famous conclusion is that there are no innate ideas, but that the mind is initially a *tabula rasa* – a blank sheet – awaiting information from the senses. This is the general position taken by empiricists, who hold that all knowledge comes through sense experience.

As mentioned earlier (page 53) in connection with Chomsky's argument for the innate ability to develop language, there needs to be a distinction made between *innate capabilities* and *innate knowledge*. Both empiricists and rationalists might hold that people can have innate capabilities, in other words that they have skills that cannot be accounted for in terms of that individual's experience. Those capabilities might, for example, by given by virtue of the way in which the species has evolved and in this sense the individual benefits from millennia of experience. In general, however, an empiricist – for whom all knowledge must come through the senses – will reject any sense of innate knowledge in the sense of knowledge of content.

# The phenomenological fallacy

In a crucial article in 1956, the philosopher U.T. Place asked 'Is consciousness a brain process?' (in *British Journal of Psychology*). He set out his task thus:

> It is argued that the problem of providing a physiological explanation of introspective observations is made to seem more difficult than it really is by the 'phenomenological fallacy', the mistaken idea that descriptions of the appearance of things are descriptions of the actual state of affairs in a mysterious internal environment.

> (Cummins and Cummins, p. 361)

Before setting out the fallacy, he makes two important points:

- That we have cognitive concepts (knowing, believing etc.) and volitional concepts (wanting, intending etc.) and that, to express consciousness, we use what amounts to an 'inner process' story. But statements about this story cannot be the same as statements about brain processes.
- That 'is' can be used in two ways – for definition and for composition. (For example: 'His home is a caravan' – this does not mean that the term 'home' is identical to or explained by the term 'caravan', it simply means that he uses a caravan as his home.)

Taking these things into account, it is clear that one can give two very different accounts of the same thing, both of which are equally valid. Thus, to use one of his examples, a cloud is also a mass of fine water droplets in suspension – from the outside we see a cloud, from within it we see this fog of water droplets: different descriptions, different locations, but the same reality.

Now, the 'phenomenological fallacy' is to suppose that, when I see a red flower, there is some image of a red flower in my brain – rather as though the inside of my head formed a miniature TV set – and that, therefore, there are two things happening at once, a pattern of neurones firing off and (at the same time) a red image.

---

**COMMENT**

Although it sounds crazy, the experience of thinking and imagining *is* a bit like watching an internal TV, so it is not unreasonable to assume that these experiences must be going on somewhere inside my head and that they cannot be the same as activity within the grey matter of my brain.

Stand back from the situation for a moment and consider exactly what it is to see a red flower. The sensory data, in the form of light of a certain wavelength reflected off the flower, enter my eye and fall on the retina. They are turned into electrical impulses that convey the information to my brain. The actual seeing of the red flower (and recognising it as a 'red flower', since I have had similar experiences in the past that have been related to the use of those two descriptive words) is – by the time it gets to my brain – a set of neurones firing.

There are not two flowers – one out there and one inside my head. There is only one flower and recognising it is a function of my whole body, involving my eyes, optic nerves and brain.

In the crude version of the fallacy – and an impression often given by a first reading of Locke and other empiricists – is that a human being is rather like a robot with TV cameras and other sensors on the outside, relaying messages to another little person (myself) on the inside. By some miracle, all the external data are conveyed into me and then set out in a form I can recognise.

But that can't work, because the little internal 'me' would also be gathering data just like the external robot and I would then require an even smaller 'real me' on the inside to unscramble and appreciate it. And so on *ad infinitum*!

---

When you 'see' something, the sensations are related to and recognised by your brain. Your consciousness is that process. To an external observer, it takes the form of eyeball, lens, retina, optic nerve and the stimulation of those sections of the brain responsible for sight. You can't see it that way, because you are the one who is doing the seeing!

Place's conclusion:

> Once we rid ourselves of the phenomenological fallacy we
> realise that the problem of explaining introspective
> observations in terms of brain processes is far from
> insuperable. We realise that there is nothing that the
> introspecting subject says about his conscious experience
> which is inconsistent with anything the physiologist might
> want to say about the brain processes which cause him to
> describe the environment and his consciousness of the
> environment in the way that he does.

---

**COMMENT**

It is difficult to overestimate the importance of recognising this
fallacy, not just for the philosophy of mind, but also for many
wider issues.

When we 'see' something, it is not 'in' the brain and projected
out as if it were in the external world, it *is* in the external world.
We do not describe our consciousness, we describe those things
of which we are conscious. There are no phenomenal properties,
other than the phenomena themselves.

Too often, because we can reconstruct images and events in our
imagination, we assume that they must 'exist' or that our concepts
are like physical bits of matter, crammed into our heads.

The brain is not some library or exhibition, where books or
pictures are lined up ready for us to compare with external
reality. It does not work in that way at all. Rather, the brain is a
phenomenally complex organ for recording, analysing,
remembering and responding to the great variety of sensations
that come its way in the form of electro-chemical impulses.

There is only one world and you are a conscious part of it for as
long as your brain is actively processing your encounter with
your environment or remembering previous encounters.

# Pragmatism and Gestalt

What is knowledge for? Why do we acquire it? These are relevant questions for the theory of knowledge, because if you know what it is for, you can understand why it is acquired in the way that it is. Pragmatists such as John Dewey (1859–1952) argued that you should not separate the content of thought from its function. People learn things because they need to know them and their need arises from problems that they face. Hence it is possible to look at the mind in terms of the way it enables people to respond to the challenges they face.

This led Dewey to develop fundamental views on the nature of education, set out in *The School and Society* (1899). Children learn best, he argued, by being presented with challenges and questions, rather than being forced to learn information that had no immediate relevance to them.

Pragmatism recognises that the mind is 'for' something. It is not occult and mysterious, but extremely useful. Its operations are not in some unobservable world, but are seen in the problem-solving process.

## Example

Squirrels can learn to negotiate various obstacles in order to get at food. Whatever thought is required to enable the squirrel to achieve this is prompted by the need to be where that food is. Similarly the tit that learns to peck away at a milk bottle top in order to get a drink is not simply responding to an abstract stimulus, but is performing an operation that has been learned in order to achieve an end result. Animal behaviour is pragmatic; it has an end in view.

It is worthwhile keeping a pragmatic approach in mind when we discuss the relationship between brain activity and consciousness. It is sometimes argued that consciousness is just a by-product of brain activity (essentially the epiphenomenalist approach – see page 22), and therefore that conscious cannot *do* anything other than what the brain does. But that is to mistake the pragmatic function of mind from its analysis. It may be true that the mind (if separated off from the brain) does not have a function – but it is the conscious mind that expresses itself through the brain activity. Taking a simple functionalist account, the brain would not know to instruct the body to raise an arm in self-protection if it were not for the sensory awareness of being about to be hit and a conscious desire to avoid injury. These (however you choose to describe them) are features of the mind and consciousness, and without them the brain would have no reason to send out the signals to raise the arm.

---

**IN OTHER WORDS**

Don't just think about how activity is produced; think about *why* it is produced. The answer to that, as evolutionary thinking suggests, is the key to understanding why the human body, brain and mind have developed as they have. To repeat an earlier analogy – to understand a car journey, look at the reason for travelling, don't try taking the engine apart!

---

Gestalt was a reaction against the early structuralist and behaviourist approaches to psychology (see pages 50 and 52). It argued that it is a fundamental mistake to assume that the mind understands things by analysing them into their constituent parts. Rather, it puts together various elements of experience in order to build up an overall picture, a whole within which the various parts can make sense. In doing this, the mind is active in interpreting and comparing experiences, it is not merely responding to individual stimuli. The mind thinks through possibilities.

Taken together, pragmatism and Gestalt theory give a very different impression of what the mind actually does, compared with the behaviourist approach. It is active, problem solving and concerned to make sense of individual sensations in terms of the whole of experience.

# 5 | PERSONAL IDENTITY AND MEMORY

Clearly, most of the issues in the philosophy of mind are concerned with, or imply, views on the nature of personal identity. The whole issue of artificial intelligence, for example, raises the question of whether a computer can be regarded as a person with an individual identity.

But in this chapter we shall look at some attempts to state clearly what is meant by being a 'person', and also at some of the key issues, such as memory and the phenomenon of worrying, which imply a clear sense of the 'being' as an individual with a definite identity.

---

### Identity and individuality

Ordinarily, the words identity and individuality are used for much the same thing – what makes a person in some way special; their character and particular appearance. In a philosophical context, however, we may need to distinguish them.

Ever since the time of Plato, thinkers have discussed how particular things relate to their overall 'form' or general description of their kind or species. In other words, how do I know that this particular thing in front of me is a tree? How does its *individuality* (being a particular size, shape and colour) relate to the general description 'tree'? So individuality is the term most appropriately used for that which distinguishes between examples of a particular kind or species. We are all 'people' but we are also all individuals, who may be distinguished from one another. By contrast, a can of beans does not have individuality – which makes it all the more surprising to us that an artist like Andy Warhol may choose to paint one.

By the same token, people change a great deal over time. The baby, adult and old person in a range of photographs may look quite different, but we are told that they are one and the same person. Personal identity therefore refers to that which remains constant for an individual, and which may therefore be used to distinguish him or her from others, who may – at this moment – share the same individual characteristics.

In the quest for personal identity, there are various aspects that can be examined, for example:

- bodily continuity
- continuity of character
- memory.

Thus, to the question 'Are you the same person who...?', one could argue first of all that you have to be the same person if there is bodily continuity. Indeed, this is the usual way of recognising someone, although it is difficult if a long time has passed since last we saw him or her. But just how much change can happen to a body for this identity to remain? The old man and the baby are physically totally different, but yet can claim to be the same person. Mentally, the person with advanced Alzheimer's disease is hardly the bright young student of years before. Names give continuity, as does genetic code – but names can be changed and genetic code is not visible; for practical purposes, therefore, we tend to supplement the basic continuity of the body with other indications of identity. Thus, one generally looks for continuity in terms of that person's character and behaviour patterns. If they have totally changed, one would be tempted to ask what had happened to cause such changes.

But, most important, a person asserts who they are and shows that they are the same person encountered earlier, by recalling events in the past. Not only do I have a sense of my own identity because of the memories I have of my own past, but I can convey that sense of identity to others by telling my personal story or by recalling shared moments. If adults meet for the first time since childhood, they can restore the bond of friendship by remembering shared childhood experiences – the person encountered in the present may look and sound totally different, but memory immediately established a deep connection.

But can a person's identity always be established and does it have a fundamental unity? Clearly, when it comes to the body, it is possible to lose a limb without thereby losing one's identity. The body is clearly divisible and some parts are going to be more crucial to personal identity than others – the successful transplant of another head would cause more problems than a transplanted liver, for example.

However, when it comes to the mind, traditional Cartesian dualism has argued that the mind is not a physical part and is therefore unextended. The implication of this is that it cannot be divided, since you can only divide that which occupies space. For Descartes, therefore, there is a single self with privileged access to its own mind.

From a materialist point of view, however, it should be possible to divide off aspects of personal identity, simply because they inhere in, or are ways of describing, something physical and the physical world is always divisible. In other words: from a dualist point of view, there is always going to be, at the core of personality and consciousness, a single mind – the 'real' me. From a materialist point of view, there is always the possibility that what I conventionally call myself is a bundle of various mental aspects, a bundle whose integrity is not assured and which might change with time.

## Personal view

One might start by considering genetic identity. Genes determine the sort of physical body that is being developed and with that development comes the learning process by which experiences are processed and mental skills and language developed. There is continuity in this physical/mental complex. In other words, from the moment of conception there has been a unique development, embodying many physical, mental and dispositional changes. Even if all the individual components of that person appear to change, the underlying process by which the complex entity is formed and developed gives it an identity.

I can take a DNA sample from an elderly person and identify him or her with the child whose trace of genetic material I have discovered with some long-lost artefact. Heraclitus said that one could not step into the same river twice, in the sense that the water of that river was constantly changing. However, that did not require that rivers should not be given a name or that one should be surprised to find it still flowing the next day. The river is a changing phenomenon, in the sense that its material is constantly flowing, but its formal identity remains.

Perhaps the individual, like the river, is a mere bundle of ever-changing strands – physical, mental, emotional, social. In an absolute (or certainly a material) sense there is no overall continuity that can be specified in terms of a fixed quality or material, but we need some way of describing an entity in process. A school remains a school even though its pupils change year by year, its staff arrive and leave and its buildings are occasionally replaced, it can even be relocated elsewhere. The school cannot therefore be defined by any physical continuity. Its identity is thus a flowing one. Why should we not consider the human being in much the same way?

# Social and role identity

In looking at social roles, we need to keep in mind, once again, the distinction between identity and individuality. Individuality is easily accounted for in terms of the theoretically infinite number of circumstances that have to come together in order to produce you as an individual. Working back from the present moment, there are the endless chances in life that have given you your experiences and therefore shaped your views.

Further back still, there was the most decisive moment for establishing your individuality – the moment of your conception. But that only took place because of a number of variables in terms of your parents meeting one another and all that followed from it, and their parents before them and so on (this was explored by

Heidegger, in his idea of the 'thrownness' of human life – we are pitched into life with a given set of facts over which we have no control and which therefore start to define who we are (see page 76). Ultimately, the whole universe has to have been exactly as it is for you to have been produced exactly as you are. Any changes anywhere in the system and everything changes at the same time.

Your individuality is therefore established by the countless variables that affect every action in life. But a society comprising individuals who did not in some way mask out some of their individuality would be chaotic. In practice, the freedom of experiencing endless possibilities is too much for people to cope with. We retreat behind masks of convention in order to get on with the business of living and dealing with others. Hence, we accept identities established by our roles within our various circles of influence.

There are, or course, many ways of identifying yourself socially:

- Through close relationships – as a son or daughter of, father or mother of, brother or sister and so on.
- As a member of a particular interest group or group of friends.
- Through a work environment – as a student in a particular faculty or as a manager or executive in a business.
- As one who holds certain views or ideas or political allegiance.
- In terms of origins – as coming from a particular country or having a rural or urban upbringing.
- As a citizen of a country or member of a race.

Each of these is appropriate in a context in which it distinguishes you from others. Thus, it is hardly worth claiming to be an earthling while on planet earth – in deep space, such an identity would take on meaning.

At different times and for different purposes, each of these will become more or less relevant. Relationships establish a sense of identity and the closer the relationship, the more significant will be its influence.

But notice what is happening as we consider social relationships. We are not trying to analyse the self, breaking it down to establish what gives it continuity and therefore identity. Rather we are considering the *whole* self as it relates to features of its environment and as it makes choices against its background.

Social identity is therefore a matter of synthesis, not of analysis. You are the sum total of the person who acts, not some inner or 'real' part that can be abstracted from the rest of your body or mind.

---

### Where are you?

Where is a friendship located? Is it in your head? Surely it cannot be, since it is a shared reality. Where is a conversation? Where is the sense of national identity or the local community? Where is your family actually located?

Physical location is relatively unimportant in establishing social identity. Rather like a web site that conveys information to anyone who accesses it, the key thing is what it says, not the particular server on which it is lodged.

It is important to keep this in mind, since it is always tempting to locate the self in the head, whereas the self, since it is social, may centre on, but is not limited by, any physical location.

---

At any one time, we may express ourselves through one or more of our relationships, which may involve both the physical and mental aspects of our existence. We act as a 'person' within the various contexts of our lives.

A philosopher who emphasised the priority of 'persons' (in the days before the rise of cognitive science, when the issue of identity was still being considered largely from a linguistic perspective, following the influence of Ryle) was P.F. Strawson (b.1919), a British philosopher known particularly for his work on the nature of identity. In 'Persons', an article published in 1958 and his book *Individuals* (1959), he argued that the concept of 'person' was such that both physical characteristics and states of consciousness could be ascribed to it. In other words, one does not have to start with minds and bodies and then see if they can be put together to form persons. Rather one starts with 'persons' and any subsequent analysis is optional.

## Note

In cognitive science, some of the old options between materialism, dualism and idealism no longer apply. Thus it is possible to be a materialist rather than a dualist (in that you reject the idea of a separate, unknowable, unextended, thinking self of the sort envisaged by Descartes) but *at the same time* you can be a mentalist (in that you do not think that a behaviourist account is adequate). The 'mind' that you subscribe to can be a matter of giving meaning and rule following, rather than some unknowable substance.

With cognitive science, there need be no problem with asking about whether a chess-playing computer has a mind of its own. You know that it has been programmed and although you cannot directly see the decisions about moves to be made, you know that the electrical impulses that do its computations about the best moves to make are taking all that information into account.

The chess computer 'thinks' what to do. We do not have to posit some occult 'self' that has come to inhabit the computer.

Why then should we have a problem with the human being who plays chess? Exactly the same process has taken place. He or she has learned rules and is now applying them with certain strategies in mind. The computer and the person are essentially performing the same function in the same way.

Of course, you could argue that the human being (although having learned the particular rules of this game) is far more than a chess-playing machine. He or she has a whole world of experience and relationships to take into account – including the decision to sit down and play chess, a decision denied to the computer, which is simply turned on when required.

But why can one not argue that the human being has, from the moment of birth, been programmed with huge numbers of instructions and ideals, goals and strategies? Some will have been taught directly, others merely inferred from observation.

Given that the computing complexity is of a quite different order, is there any 'in principle' difference between the two situations? And, if not, what does that say about personal identity and the distinctiveness (if any) of humans?

Clearly, from what we have been exploring in this section, 'persons' exist in a social context. Their identity is not established by analysis of attributes, but by examining how they relate to others, contribute to friendships, family groups, nations and so on. The concept of person and personal identity emerges only in this holistic context.

# Memory

As we have already seen, memory is an important factor in establishing identity. You are what you are because you have learned from the past, your values and attitudes are shaped by your experience – and that depends on memory. A person without a memory might still have a whole variety of skills, but would otherwise be quite lost. Without memory there is no recognition and without recognition it is difficult to respond to whatever is presented to the senses.

Memory is private. David Hume saw memory in terms of a sequence of private images running through one's head. If I say I remember something, it is difficult for someone else to contradict me, unless there is evidence that I physically could not have been where I claim to remember having been. Police, in interviewing a suspect, will be challenging his or her claimed memory on exactly those grounds.

Clearly, much of what we remember is quite unconscious or perhaps the time it takes the memory to access the information is so short that the mind does not have opportunity to reflect upon it. I do not have to stop and think before giving my name, if asked.

There is also a difference between remembering skills (how to walk), logical or mathematical principles ($2 \times 2 = 4$) and remembering particular events ('Where were you at the time the crime was committed?').

But just because we may have privileged access to our own memories does not mean that we are infallible. Two people may give very different accounts of a meeting, since memories are selective, including those things that are deemed significant and ignoring those that are not.

We shall therefore look briefly at three aspects of memory – related to knowledge, to therapy and to identity.

## Knowing and remembering

A person suffering temporary memory loss generally cannot remember specific things – such as where he or she lives. This is very disorientating, because the reliability of memory is what gives our lives continuity. Contrariwise, a person with memory loss is still able to know that $2 + 2 = 4$ and is still able to use his or her native language. In other words, there are fundamental features of the way our minds work, logically and linguistically, which appear to be instinctive and not dependent upon specific acts of memory. Learning a skill is a matter of acquiring an ability to perform certain manipulations of concepts in the present. Once that skill is acquired, the actual circumstances through which it was learned may generally be forgotten. Remembering our first teacher is different in kind from remembering the words that he or she taught.

By the same token, if we move away from specific skills of mathematics, logic or language, it is clear that memory lays down in the mind various levels of skills – emotional and social abilities, for example – that serve as a resource for us later. Thus, the way we learn to handle difficult situations, perhaps with brothers or sisters in childhood, may be a training ground for later adult negotiations with other people.

A key question remains. Are we – as Locke classically claimed – born with *tabula rasa*, a blank sheet upon which our experience will soon start to write? Or are we born with certain innate tendencies and abilities? If the latter, are these deterministic for our life – rather as DNA determines the colour of our eyes – or do we have a measure of control over them?

Is it possible that we can 'remember' something that we have not ourselves experienced? Is there a form of collective memory? Or, following Plato, do we remember fundamental realities (the forms) from a life before this present birth? Clearly, memory and identity are closely linked in these issues.

## Memory and therapy

As we go through life, our thoughts, emotions and attitudes are shaped by our experiences. Some of the influences upon our present view of life are conscious, others (particularly from the earliest stages of life) are unconscious. In either case, what appears to be happening is that experience leads to patterning. An experience (whether pleasant or painful) leads to the anticipation of what will happen to us when we encounter something similar in the future. Hence, we have a pattern by which to assess the present and anticipate the future. If a particular aspect of life has brought us trauma in the past, we will (consciously or unconsciously) carry that pattern of expectation with us.

It is the ability to remember the past that makes therapy effective in changing attitudes and emotions in the present. If it were not for memory, we would not be able to learn or adapt our behaviour in line with experience. Clearly, this is most clearly illustrated in the process of counselling or psychotherapy. It is in exploring the past that we find the roots of our present emotional states.

Now, clearly, the past cannot be changed. Neither, of course, is it any use to pretend that past events did not happen – it is exactly the tendency to repress painful experiences that leads to psychological dysfunction later in life. All the therapist or analyst attempts to do is to expose the past and allow it to become 'patterned' differently. In other words, brought out into the open, the adult mind is able to interpret that experience differently and is therefore less influenced by the previous ways in which it has been interpreted, generally from the perspective of a young and vulnerable child.

## Memory and identity

Memory appears to work on a need-to-know basis. We are not consciously aware of the whole of our past all the time, that would be to give our awareness an information overload, but as we need to remember things – our name as we go to sign, where we have left the parked car, where we live or where we had set out to go and the route by which to get there – so that information generally appears available to our conscious mind. An acting subject makes choices, behaves in predictable ways and generally displays a particular identity, because of his or her memory. Predictability simply refers to the likelihood that a person will remember what has already happened and will act accordingly. The person who previously has disliked the taste of a certain food is likely to decline it when it is offered.

A case can therefore be made for saying that our memory provides an ever-expanding range of past experiences that convey values and meanings, helping us to make wise choices in the present. Memory provides a background to all our thoughts and actions – a background which Heidegger (see page 76) saw as particularly important in shaping our existential decisions.

Returning to the consideration of therapy for a moment, all we need to see for our purposes here is that the way in which therapy works illustrates the function of memory as setting patterns of present interpretation. It is easiest to see this in the case of those who have been severely traumatised and whose present life is hampered by those past events. But the process that is illustrated by therapy must surely apply to everyone — that our personal identity is shaped by the mapping and interpreting function (with past experiences giving us patterns for present interpretation) and the key to this is memory.

Hence, identity is constantly shaped by experience and access to experience is given by memory. And this, of course, is why some memories are vivid and others are vague – indeed, why most things are not consciously remembered at all. Memory selects according to significance and significance is set down in terms of patterns of experience and response. We remember those things that we need to keep in mind for our future protection. If I experience something painful, my memory is activated in order that I can avoid a similar thing in the future. The past is therefore selected by significance not by random access. And the ordering of that significance defines the nature of my personality.

# Worrying

The ability to worry seems to be an interesting test of mind/body theories. The worrier is not concerned with actual situations, but with potential situations.

In a sense, there is an absolute cure for worrying: if something cannot be changed, then there seems no point in worrying about it, but if it can be changed, then there is no point in worrying and one should simply set about changing it.

Now, what exactly is the worrier doing? Why can't he take the simple advice and recognise that worrying does not actually solve problems?

The worrier is using the facility of memory to remember past problems or accounts of past problems given by others. In the light of these, the future is contemplated and problems anticipated. The worrier then turns the possibilities over and over in his mind. The worrier is said to be 'preoccupied' and the process of worrying can be quite exhausting. He might frown or look distant and it is clear that the source of that vagueness is not given by the present environment or situation in which the person finds himself.

Now, one might be tempted to ask (along with the behaviourists) whether worrying is to be identified with the distant gaze, the knitted brow and the preoccupation with a limited range of ideas or situations.

Worrying is not an activity brought about through exhaustion, having a furrowed brow or staring out into space in a vacant measure. It is an activity that *causes* all those things. If a behaviourist were right about mental actions being convenient names for material processes, then it would make no sense to say that someone was worried but that he had completely disguised the fact.

If observational data are all there is, there is no difference between 'looking worried' and 'being worried'. We all know that it is possible to hide some of one's feelings and act calmly while living on the brink of some panic attack – most actors about to go on stage could confirm that.

But worrying is also a problem for any epiphenomenal approach to mind. If mental states are simply a by-product of physical states, then what has triggered the worrying? It cannot be accounted for in terms of a response to present stimulus, since the cause of the worrying is imaginary – potential situations, rather than actual ones.

Worrying does, however, show the importance of the evolutionary function of mind. Thinking about how to deal with potentially difficult situations is, as we saw earlier (page 58), a feature that gives members of a species a definite advantage and therefore marks a direction for evolutionary advance. Worrying is an extreme version of the very technique that early man needed to develop in order to overcome problems – the ability to visualise potential situations and consider how to deal with them.

# Zombies

What would happen if you could use a machine to duplicate every cell in your body and in effect create another person that was physically identical to yourself, with all the usual functions of movement and so on, but with no mind? Such a being is referred to in philosophical discussions as a zombie. Now the key question is this: How can you tell the difference between a zombie and a normal human being? In other words, how – once you have given a full physical description (which would be identical for both you and zombie you) – do you start to describe the *person*?

Of course, if zombies are literally possible, then the case for dualism is complete – for one could show exactly what it is like to have all the physical attributes but without a mind. But, surely, even if it is possible simply to *imagine* what a zombie would be like (and, surely, everyone can imagine that) then it implies that we do actually understand people in dualist terms.

---

**Mindless**!

We all have a notion of what a mindless dummy would be like – and if we are cruel enough to refer to a work colleague in this way, we know what sort of characteristics (or lack of them) have led us to make the comment! So, whether or not we agree with the philosophical arguments in favour of dualism, for practical purposes we do know how to ascribe physical qualities and to comment when mental qualities appear to be absent.

---

Of course, the kind of dualism that the dummy illustrates could well be a dualism of properties, rather than of essences. The mindless dummy behind that desk has a complete set of physical properties and a total absence of mental ones.

Now there is a clear distinction between thinking that it should be possible for something to exist and knowing that it exists. I may have an idea of a zombie – for all the reasons just given – but that does not mean that a zombie actually exists. How could I tell if the apparently human object in front of me is a person or a zombie?

A zombie, in the philosophical sense, is identical to a normal human being. Thus every conceivable test that could be put to the zombie would be returned as if done by a normal human. But what the zombie does not have, apparently, is the inner experience of a mind – *but that is unknowable anyway*.

The argument that, because we can conceive of a zombie existing, we must accept some form of dualism, actually amounts to this:

- You can experience your own mind.
- You cannot experience someone else's mind.
- Someone else's mind is only known insofar as it is mediated by language or action.
- Such mediation is equally open to zombies, if the zombie is programmed accordingly.
- Therefore it is no more possible to prove that this thing in front of you is a zombie than to prove that it is an intelligent human being.

All the argument shows is that mind is experienced rather than seen by physical analysis; it is always possible to imagine an entity that is totally physically analysed without having any notion of it having a mind.

In other words, the zombie argument is a thought experiment, showing how very different our ideas of mind and matter are. But that is all it amounts to. In the real world, we could never know if zombies exist, for (other than in our imagination) we have no independent knowledge of other minds.

## COMMENT

Artificial intelligence makes what is, in effect, a rather banal contribution to issues of the nature of self and consciousness. Namely that, given the ability to make a computer with the same capacity as the human brain and given input sensors and output devices equal to those of human senses and bodily functions, then that computer (embodied in a robot, in order to receive and respond to stimuli) would be indistinguishable from a human being.

But what has been achieved by this? In a way, it gets back to the issue of zombies. To claim that it might be possible to produce an exact replica of a human being and then say that such a replica would be indistinguishable from the original is to make a hypothetical claim that, in effect, can yield nothing by way of information about the self other than what can be gained by observing ordinary human beings.

It would be necessary, of course, to give the replica a history, complete with memories. It would need to take as long to produce it as it takes to grow a human being, so that it learned what it was like to experience every stage of life.

In other words, if one could make a human being exactly as human beings are made, then the result would be indistinguishable from human beings. But of course! And the problems of understanding the mind and consciousness would remain exactly as they are now.

The issues of zombies and artificial intelligence, with the possibility of constructing and defining human identity and consciousness, come down to this: If we could construct a world exactly like this one, then it would be exactly like this one. Which, as a contribution to the understanding of mind, is trivial.

# 6 KNOWLEDGE OF OTHER MINDS

We tend to assume that we can know another person, because we can try to imagine what it must be to be that other person. We assume that their mind is like our own. But what if they are quite different? In an article in 1974, Thomas Nagel famously asked 'What is it like to be a bat?' and the answer we give to that question is most significant.

First of all, if we simply try to imagine that we (with all our existing faculties) are living as a bat, then the situation seems quite bizarre. So, for example, I find my way around by bouncing high-frequency sound waves off nearby objects and analysing the echoes that are reflected back to me. Now, what can it mean to experience objects as, effectively, echoes? The answer is that the problem is only apparent because we are a human pretending to be a bat. In practice, the bat has always 'seen' objects through the echoes it receives – therefore what it is aware of is not the echoes themselves, but the object that its brain has constructed out of those echoes.

What is the implication of this? Clearly, I see objects by analysing the light waves that are focused on the retina at the back of each eye and which are then transmitted to the brain in the form of two sets of electrical impulses, which the brain sorts out in order to give stereoscopic vision. But we do not 'see' neurones firing in my brain or electrical impulses being turned off and on or the light waves striking the retina. Unless I want to stop and analyse the process, all I actually experience is that at which I am looking. The same must be true for the way in which the bat 'sees' things.

The conclusion Nagel came to was that no amount of information could ever tell us what it is like to be a bat. (Just as no amount of information about the eyeball or optic nerve is ever going to be able to tell us what it is like to see.) What something is like can only be *appreciated* from the point of view of the creature concerned.

**IN OTHER WORDS**

Even if I know that an experience only takes place when there is activity in a particular part of my brain, that does not imply that the experience is identical with that activity, in the sense that to know the one is to know the other. A neurobiologist recording the brain activity would not be able to see what I see. The instruments might show that something was being experienced, but not the qualitative feel of that experience.

This has important implications, as we shall see later, for the general area of understanding what it means to be conscious. But it is also significant for our purpose here – the knowledge of other minds. Clearly, I cannot come to know what it is for another person to be conscious through analysing the systems in which that consciousness is embodied. However detailed and precise the knowledge I get about neurone firing in the brain of the person I am examining, it is never going to be the same as the other person's experience. To return to the familiar image: you cannot discover the purpose of a journey by examining the workings of a motorcar engine.

## The structuralist approach

Early psychologists (e.g. Wundt and Titchener) hoped to understand the structure of the mind and to explain it in physical terms. They were generally opposed to the Cartesian dualism that made the mind inaccessible to physical investigation and wanted to show that thinking was essentially a physical process.

They assumed that the process of thinking was based on images and that images came from simple sensations. Hence, if the process of thought could be analysed into the very simplest of sensations, its structure could be revealed. But how were these sensations to be known? Clearly, the only way was for people to describe what they experienced, breaking down that experience into its component parts.

The process of doing this was laborious. The people giving their descriptions could not simply say that they saw, for example, a red flower. Rather, they had to break down exactly the quality of colour, shape, smell, touch etc. that added up to the overall experience of the flower. The assumption was made that the mind simply put all these simple sensations together in order to construct the concept 'red flower'.

But there was a huge problem with this whole approach. It depended on the skill of the person being interviewed in being able to analyse experience accurately. What was more, there seemed to be no way of checking the accuracy of their accounts. What if they were mistaken? What if they were lying? What if (as often happened) two people gave different analyses of identical stimuli?

In the end, these 'structuralists', as they became known, listed 44,000 elementary sensations, but their whole task failed because there was no way of knowing if any of them were in fact correct.

The whole problem was that of knowledge of other minds. The psychologists were totally dependent on what the subjects said to them. They had no other way of knowing if the person had actually had a particular sensation. Introspection was their only method of working, because only the person actually having that sensation could possibly know and describe it. Nobody else was in a position to challenge that, because nobody else could know what was going on in that person's mind.

It was against that background that the behaviourists (e.g. Pavlov, Watson and Skinner) presented stimulus and response as the basis of their work. Responses could be observed and measured in a way that allowed psychology to follow the norms of the physical sciences. They were no longer dependent on unproved reports from an experiencing subject, since their subjects now exhibited patterns of behaviour that could be measured.

Hence, behaviourism thought that it had got round the problem of knowledge of other minds by saying, in effect, that there should be no reference to 'internal' states of mind at all. Psychology was only concerned with the prediction of observable behaviour – of how people and animals learned and responded to things. Whatever 'thought' might have taken place between stimulus and response was irrelevant. What counted was what could be observed. For them, consciousness either did not exist or – if it did – it was an epiphenomenon (see page 22), produced by brain activity.

The problem of the knowledge of other minds (or rather, the impossibility of observing the workings of another mind) has, therefore shaped much of the development of psychology as a science.

Science depends on evidence and if there is no way of gaining independently checkable and objective evidence about the workings of the mind, then there can be no science of mind. That was the fundamental problem facing psychology.

# Brains

Everyone agrees that, when mental activity is going on, there is also physical activity going on in that person's brain. To describe someone as 'brain dead' indicates that there is absolutely no brain function (which could be measured, since it involves electrical activity) and therefore that there is no chance of a return to consciousness.

We saw earlier that a materialist (as opposed to dualist) viewpoint is one that identifies mental operations with brain activity. But here there is a fundamental problem, the classical account of which is known as 'Leibniz' gap (see page 21).

In section 17 of his *Monadology*, Leibniz considers the problem of how one might examine the process of perception. He argues that perception cannot be described in terms of a mechanism. Even if one could construct a mechanism that could think and feel, on examining that mechanism it would be like – in his analogy – entering a mill. One would see only pieces of mechanism that push against one another – but one would not be able to see the thought or sensation itself.

In other words, there is a gap between the concepts we use in describing physical mechanisms and the words we use to describe thought and sensation.

Thus, even if we were convinced that thought was identical to brain activity, the language used to describe that activity would not be the same as that which describes thought. Language about mental operation cannot be reduced to that about brain function, even if it is shown that the brain function is the occasion of a mental operation taking place.

This has immediate implications for the considerations of both brains and artificially constructed brains in the form of computers. Even if we have a computer which appears to 'think' the thoughts are not the same as the operations of that computer. There will always be a gap between saying that this is what the computer is doing and saying what (or if) the computer is thinking. Hence, unless you are an eliminative materialist (see page 34) and believe that they are one and the same thing, even a full and detailed knowledge of neurobiology would not allow you to know what it is like to experience the workings of another mind.

# Ways of knowing

Taking a dualistic view of minds and bodies, it is impossible to have direct knowledge of another mind. You can get to know a person well, understanding his or her words, actions, writings and body language, but you cannot get direct access to their mind. If, following Descartes, minds are unextended, knowledge of other minds cannot come through ordinary sense experience, but must be inferred by analogy with one's own mind. I know what it is like to be me – I know that, when I speak, I am expressing what is in my mind. Therefore, I assume that, when another person speaks, his or her words are similarly the product of what is in his or her mind.

Of course, if you turn from dualism and follow the views of Gilbert Ryle, there is no problem. There is no 'Ghost in the Machine'; what we mean by mind is the intelligent and communicative abilities of that other person. It is a description of what they do and say. If I know his or her actions, words and so on, then I know his or her mind; the two things are one and the same.

But self-knowledge is always going to be a problem for those who follow Ryle's view. If mental phenomena are simply covert ways of describing physical actions or dispositions to act, then my knowledge of myself is not qualitatively different from my knowledge of others. I notice that I have smiled and therefore come to the conclusion that it is appropriate to call myself 'happy'. I find myself jumping up and down and holding my leg and I assume that I have suffered 'pain'.

This, of course, is nonsense. Those physical actions are made in response to a subjective experience. Where other people are concerned, because I cannot have direct access to their subjective experiences, I have to infer them from the resulting actions, gestures words and so on. In my own case, however, the subjective experience is not inferred from anything, it is experienced directly.

To say that someone else is happy, one needs empirical evidence – of smiling or saying that he or she is happy, of skipping down the road or whatever. That evidence, by analogy with one's own experience, gives one reasonable justification for saying that the other person is 'happy'. In the case of one's own happiness, by way of contrast, knowledge of that emotion is immediate and direct; no external evidence is needed.

But clearly, language is shared and a word needs to have the same meaning when applied to others as well as to oneself. This led P.F. Strawson (particularly in an article entitled 'Persons' in 1958) to argue that the concept of a person or individual is a primitive one. If the same thing can be predicated of others on the basis of observable evidence and of myself on the basis of subjective experience, then there must be a sense of the person that is deeper than the conventional dualistic division between the inner self and external body. In other words, the idea of person includes both the physical and the non-physical. Once the idea of person is placed centrally in this debate, then the use of language both for myself and others makes more sense – its ascription can use different criteria, but its meaning remains constant. (This type of argument in favour of a primitive notion of 'person' had also been put forward by A.J. Ayer in *The Concept of a Person*, 1955.) Predicates that imply a person (e.g. 'is happy'), go beyond those that simply give a physical description (e.g. 'is thin'), in that they presuppose that the object to which we ascribe them has states of consciousness.

In other words, although the ways of knowing are very different, we have a primitive sense of a person which justifies the ascription of personal predicates both to ourselves and to others. I know when I am in pain and I see when someone else is in pain – and the reasons for knowing it are very different in the two cases – but, if we hold that the idea of 'person' is primitive, then we may assume that to say that you are in pain and that I am in pain refer to the same experience.

In many ways that seems quite obvious, but, at a time when justification for ascribing predicates (and the dominance of linguistic philosophy in general) was paramount, it broke the impasse of having very different criteria for ascribing the same predicates to oneself and others.

There are other possible ways to know another mind. One of these is *telepathy*, and the detailed arguments about whether or not it is possible are beyond the scope of this book. It may be that there is some direct but unconscious way of ascertaining what another person is thinking. Certainly there is evidence that some people, particularly close relatives, claim such knowledge and such evidence needs to be assessed on exactly the same terms as any other scientific hypothesis. Or it may be that what passes for telepathy is in fact a form of fast and unconscious intuition from the conscious or unconscious visual clues that the other person gives to the content of his or her mind.

More obvious than intuition is the fact that, in the ordinary run of things, we generally know other people through *language*. We know what they are thinking and indeed that they are capable of thought, because they tell us. Sometimes we have a problem, in that the person we want to get to know cannot speak our language. We may have to make do with sign language. Similarly with higher forms of animal life – a dog may know a few words and may respond, by wagging its tail or skulking away sheepishly, according to whether it identifies our words as of praise or blame.

But how can we tell whether another person has a process of thinking that is like our own? I have a string of words going through my head. Do others have the same? Generally speaking, except for moments when we just sit and stare, we have words and concepts running in our minds. What would it be like to have a mind but no language? Could we think without language of some sort?

But if language is the medium through which the process of reflective consciousness takes place – in other words, that to reflect on something is to use language about it – then which comes first, mind or language?

Do we grow mentally through language and communication or do we evolve brains and then find that the natural use to put them to is communication and language?

It is clear that the development of mind has gone hand in hand with the increase in brain volume. But which has produced which? Is mental development something that takes place *between* people rather than simply in their heads? If so, the expanding brain is simply, in ordinary evolutionary terms, the increase in those members of the species who have the advantage of more brainpower.

If language and communication – with all the social advantages that have come with it – are key to the increase in mental capacity, then the computer model of mind is rather lacking. There is no point in building bigger and bigger computers in the hope that eventually the processors will rival the human brain and then suddenly expect it to be brilliant. Clearly, the process of developing brilliance is the right communication. To be cut off from the world of thought and language is to be stunted. Hence the 'mental' world need not be located between the ears. True, that is the locus of each individual's experienced share of the mental world – that is, the machine that uses the energy to fuel the effort of thought – but the mental activity itself is far from physically located. The individual thinking alone may be private now, but the activity of thinking is not separable from the rest of the world – for all the concepts being displayed have been acquired socially; that is the nature of language.

Since the experience of consciousness includes much of the 'inner dialogue' of thought, as well as those moments when we are actually speaking or writing, it is clear that our most private thoughts are borrowed from the public domain. Hence our unverifiable ability to explain our thoughts – we use language to express something that takes place largely due to language.

**The bicameral mind**

One of the most fascinating books on the development of consciousness, primarily in the sense of self-awareness, is *The Origin of Consciousness in the Breakdown of the Bicameral Mind* by Julian Jaynes (Houghton Mifflin, 1977; Penguin, 1990). It is relevant here because it argues that there was a time (around 3,000 years ago) when people started to become aware of themselves in a new way, entering into dialogues with themselves as they decided what they should do. Prior to that there was a sense of external forces speaking directly and controlling human activity.

Quite apart from the fascinating questions this raises for the philosophy of mind, it is also of interest for those considering the phenomenon of religion, for Jaynes' theory would suggest that present belief in God or the gods is a residual feature of that more primitive state of human consciousness when humans were far more aware than now of apparently 'external' voices commanding their attention.

# Are we alone?

Clearly, if the only mind we can know directly is our own, then we may doubt that any other mind exists, since all we can experience of others is what our senses detect in terms of their bodies, gestures, words and actions. We cannot touch other minds directly. Such a lonely view is termed *solipsism*, and this is the fate of those who think of the mind as an unknowable 'ghost' – the caricature of Descartes presented by Ryle.

But what does this really mean? I cannot know exactly what it is like to be that other person, I cannot have that person's experiences, but to suggest that means I cannot know another mind is to limit the mind to the most obvious of dualist caricatures – the private, unknowable world between another person's ears.

We may look another person in the eyes and sense we are looking into their deepest thoughts, probing for signs of sincerity or duplicity. But what is actually there, behind those eyes? Nothing but the soft grey matter of the brain. And all the possible scientific equipment available will do no more than show in what parts of that grey matter energy is being used.

At one level, therefore, the solipsist argument seems to have force. The world I experience is not the same as my experience of it; and if someone else examined me at this moment, they would not be able to 'see' what I am experiencing, only the physical organs that enable me to do so. Therefore, although solipsism seems quite unacceptable, the argument in favour of it is quite straightforward and logical. Happiness is not the same thing as smiling; I assume that others are happy, but I may be fooled. Any actor could present to me a completely bogus set of mental characteristics.

---

**COMMENT**

Shakespeare commented that all the world is a stage. True, I may stand on it and play the various parts I am given and others do the same. The tragedy is that, if solipsism is true, we only ever know the *parts* others play, never our fellow actors.

---

Hence there is no way that I can know another mind for certain. I merely look out at the world of my experience and, by analogy, assume that other bodies represent persons with minds. If nothing but certainty will do in my quest to know other minds, then I am alone in my world and so are you!

# Knowing me

Descartes took the view that we are aware of everything that is in our own mind. Since the mind is a thinking thing, he argued, nothing could be in the mind that is not a thought. In other words, he did not take what we would now think of as unconscious states into account. If the mind is simply the organ of thinking, then its thoughts must be known. It made no sense to say that we could be aware of something that was not a thought.

It is a feature of dualism that one has immediate and certain knowledge of one's own mind, but not of other people's. This is the 'privileged access' view that was attacked by Gilbert Ryle.

However, just because – following Descartes – I am aware of myself as a thinking being and cannot be persuaded that I do not exist while I am aware of my own thought, that does not allow me to *define* myself simply in those terms. I may be forced to acknowledge that I am a thinking being, but I sense that I am a lot more besides.

Not all philosophers were as certain about themselves as Descartes. Both Hume and Kant, when they tried to interrogate their own minds, found only a procession of particular thoughts and experiences. The self generally remained *elusive*. In other words, it is clear that parts of me may be amputated without altering my sense of identity; I can speak of 'my hand' or 'my foot'. But I can also speak of 'my body' and 'my mind' – as though neither physical nor mental aspects of myself were *all* that I am.

This should not be surprising. Just as Nagel challenged us to think about what it might be like to be a bat and showed that a description was not the same as 'what it was like to be', so it is obvious that the various bits and pieces of myself are part of a description (they *objectify* parts of me – looking at them, as it were, from the outside) and therefore cannot show 'what it is like to be me'.

---

**Introspection**

Remember, as you consider the use of introspection in order to show the contents of your own mind, that there is no way in which you can have the validity of what you claim challenged. Nobody can compare what you say with the reality of what you are experiencing, simply because nobody else has access to that experience. Your introspection has to be taken at face value and believed or simply discarded.

---

# Are you in my world?

One thing is abundantly clear at this stage in the argument: any attempt to give an objective description of the self as 'I' is going to end in frustration. Whenever we take part of ourselves and describe it, as part of the world that others can experience, the 'I' vanishes from the description. As we have just seen, I can speak of 'my mind', 'my emotions' as well as 'my body'. There is always an 'I' of 'what it is like to be me' that is over and above whatever is being described. Whatever is in my world, I stand back from it, even if I acknowledge it as 'mine'.

At the same time, I recognise that I cannot directly know another 'I', but have to infer it from the phenomena I encounter in my world. One philosopher who has taken this issue very seriously is Wittgenstein (1889–1951).

Just as other people cannot directly experience the 'I' that is more than my body and its words and actions but have to infer it, so they are not literally part of the world that I experience: I cannot know them directly. In some way, whether it can be justified or not, we know others only through a complex process of inference from their language and actions and we do so by analogy with our immediate knowledge of ourselves. There is a real sense (the argument for solipsism) that the self is alone in the world of experience. But more than that – *the self is not even 'in' the world.*

In his famous work *Tractatus*, in which he looks at the meaning of statements, the way in which they may be verified and the way they correspond to external reality, Wittgenstein said the following:

> The philosophical I is not the man, not the human body or the human soul of which psychology treats, but the metaphysical subject, the limit – not part of the world
>
> (5:641)

For Wittgenstein, 'The world is all that is the case' – in other words, our language pictures the external world, so that the limits of our language are also the limits of our world. This can bring comfort. Thus, for example, death is not part of the world; we never actually experience our own death. At death, we simply cease to experience anything at all.

It is therefore illogical to say what *cannot* exist – for to do that you would have to get beyond the limits of the world. We cannot get outside the world and look back in! But all language refers to this world that we experience here and now. So, if the subject self is not part of the world, we cannot speak or even think about it directly:

What we cannot think, that we cannot think: we cannot therefore say what we cannot think.

(5:61)

*Tractatus* is a notoriously difficult book, because its strings of short, numbered aphorisms require a great deal of unpacking to yield their full meaning. What we can say, however, is that Wittgenstein has probed the limits of what can be said meaningfully. The world is coextensive with what we can think, know and say. We cannot set its limits, because we cannot get outside it to observe those limits. We do know, however, that in a real sense 'we' are not part of our world – the philosophical 'self' is the limit of the world.

---

**IN OTHER WORDS**

I start where my world stops; you start where my world stops. Whatever I say about you becomes part of my world and cannot therefore be the philosophical 'you'. Whatever I analyse of you (or of me) becomes part of my world. You are therefore always on the borderline of my experience, in that crossing between what can be said and what cannot. As I get to know 'you', more and more of what you are is allowed to enter my world – I hear your words, see your actions and gestures. The 'you' I know and describe to others is fully in my world – but in a literal sense, you yourself remain beyond the limit of my world.

---

Some philosophers (e.g. Churchland) argue that we do not actually come to know other minds either by means of analogy or as the result of some deductive conclusion from experience, but simply because the assumption that there are other minds, similar to our own, as a *reasonable explanatory hypothesis*. In other words, if you assume it to be the case, then it makes it reasonably straightforward to predict the behaviour of other people. If you do not assume that there are other minds, then you have to go through some fairly complicated sorts of reasoning in order to determine how you should treat people who are known to the senses, but whose minds remain unknown to you.

# 7 | FREE WILL AND ACTION

If my mind is no more than a by-product of processes going on in my brain (see page 22), or if the eliminative materialist (page 34) or behaviourist (page 30) understanding of the mind is correct, then whatever I do is determined by the process of cause and effect that operates throughout the physical universe. But does that square with my own experience? And do I see others as totally conditioned by their physical circumstances or do I see them as free agents? And if none of us has free will, can we ever be held morally responsible for what we do?

The issue of free will is a key one in the philosophy of mind, touching on issues concerned with science, religion and ethics. To a large measure, my understanding of freedom will colour my understanding of the nature of the self. I decide to do something, and then do it. That is a most obvious feature of sentient life; our thoughts lead to actions. But how it that possible? If dualism is correct, how can something that is not physical bring about changes in the physical world? Where is the mechanism that inserts a physical cause corresponding to the mental decision to act? This is a fundamental question for any dualist approach to the mind and it was of concern to Descartes, who saw the point of interaction as being the pineal gland (see page 18).

## Freedom and physical causality

The problem is that, in any scientific analysis of physical nature, the chain of causality spreads outwards and backwards from any physical event, everything arises in dependence upon other things, and there appear to be no 'gaps' in the chain of causation into which the 'mental' input can be inserted. The physical world seems to be seamless and to give a complete explanation of action, without the need for minds at all.

But do we need to worry about 'gaps' at all? The caricature of the complete physical explanation of the world tends to focus on the contact between physical bodies – and that was exactly the physics with which Descartes worked.

One thing that needs to be appreciated here is how very limited Descartes' concept of physical causation was. We should not assume that Descartes had what was to become the later Newtonian view of science. Far from it. His mechanics depended on contact. Thus 'A' could only influence 'B' if there could be shown to be some direct physical contact between them. Newtonian physics, by contrast, accepted the idea of forces, namely the influence of bodies on one another through fields of force, acting at a distance. Hence, in looking at issues of freedom, and thus of the mechanisms by which mental activity can influence physical activity, we should not be concerned to find a replacement for the pineal gland – even Newtonian physics went beyond that. Does Newtonian physics leave open the possibility that the mind may also be a non-material cause of movement? After all, you can't 'observe' gravity.

**IN OTHER WORDS**

Gravity does not 'exist' in the sense of being an object among other objects. Gravity is simply the way of describing a force that acts between bodies, itself the product of the size and proximity of those bodies. Therefore, there wouldn't be gravity holding me down, if it were not for the fact that I am a small physical body standing on a much larger physical body, namely the planet. But the 'gravity' which describes that downward force, is not a 'third' material thing over and above the planet and my physical body.

Similarly, every body has its 'centre of gravity', which is useful for calculating the way in which the force of gravity will act, but gravity itself acts across the whole body. I cannot have an operation to remove my centre of gravity – it is not physical in that sense.

Thinking of mental causation as an invisible and non-material force, like gravity, at least gets rid of the cruder images of causal chains without gaps.

Thus Newton, by introducing action at a distance, left open the possibility that, if invisible and non-material forces like gravity could move bodies, there could be a similar invisible and non-material mental force causing intelligent beings to act.

However, as science has developed it is generally accepted that there are only four basic forces, the strong and weak nuclear, the electromagnetic and gravity (or three, if the weak nuclear and electromagnetic are taken together). It is generally held that one or more of these forces must cause all physical movement. Hence the idea of 'vital spirits' or the like has generally been rejected, along with the idea that a special force 'emerges' from specific, complex arrangements of matter – as, for example, in the brain and nervous systems of sentient beings.

Which brings us back to an updated form of Descartes' problem – that we still have to find some way in which mental activity can lead to physical activity.

A very clear definition (and one that relates closely to his overall thesis about the failure of Descartes' dualism) comes from Gilbert Ryle in *The Concept of Mind*:

> The problem of the Freedom of the Will was the problem how to reconcile the hypothesis that minds are to be described in terms drawn from the categories of mechanics with the knowledge that higher-grade human conduct is not of a piece with the behaviour of machines.

In other words, what Ryle and others have pointed out is that human activity becomes problematic if we use the analogy of the machine to try to understand human activity and they therefore try to find some way of getting an additional causal factor into the mechanistic chain, a factor which will allow people a measure of freedom in what they do.

So the first thing to avoid in this discussion is the temptation to see the body as a mechanistic chain that needs to have just one more causal factor within it – we can't just try to find a modern-day version of Descartes' pineal gland.

The other thing to observe is that the mind *influences but does not determine* physical action. I may, for example, choose to fly or to jump 30 feet into the air – but choosing to do so is as far as I am able to get with either aspiration. There are always going to be physical constraints. Whatever is done is in line with the normal actions of physical bodies. The effect of the mind is to select between the almost infinite number of possible physical actions that may take place.

Thus, I choose which word to utter. My tongue is equally physically capable of articulating 'yes' or 'no'. In terms of physical causation, there is nothing to choose between them. Hence, even if – within a strictly mechanistic picture of the physical environment – the physical act of articulating either word is causally linked (the action requires the movement of muscles in the tongue, lips and jaw, linked to neurones firing in the brain and chemical messages to trigger the muscle movement), the fact that such links produce one word rather than another is not thereby physically determined.

---

### Told you so!

Even if the tongue is capable of either reply and the scientific understanding of the action permits either word, there is still a sense in which my reply may be determined. That is, someone who knows me well, having observed my replies to questions on many other occasions, may be able to predict accurately whether I will reply yes or no. In other words, we may be psychologically or sociologically determined.

But we have already seen that the sense of personal identity and individual character is built up through the accumulation of experience and the patterns of understanding and evaluation that come from them. But such patterning and evaluation are not part of a physical process, they are a key function of mind – they are part of the way we experience the world. That factor is only determinist if we can never change, never develop as individuals and never benefit from therapy!

---

Modern science does not have a predetermined concept of what counts as 'body'. Rather, 'body' is whatever is discovered to be physically the case. The scientist does not therefore draw a line and suggest that everything beyond it must have some occult cause, to be found in a quasi-mechanical but non-extended mental realm. Rather, whatever phenomenon is observed becomes a valid object of study. Just because a set of physical actions – e.g. language, accompanied by gestures of movements – is explicable only in terms of the overall life of a complex being that displays features of consciousness and volition does not make it occult. Any explanation may require new concepts or a new approach, but such 'mental' actions should not be, in principle, inexplicable.

Thus, for example, if a national catastrophe (e.g. an economic slump) coincides with specific actions (e.g. the suicide of leading figures in the business world), the suggestion that the former led to the latter is not occult – simply that it is the influence of social forces which are not of the crude physical contact sort that Descartes assumed.

---

**COMMENT**

It seems remarkable that, whereas within the world of science, Cartesian contact mechanics quickly gave way to Newtonian physics, Descarte's theory seems to have continued to influence the formulation of the mind/body problem, right through to the time of Gilbert Ryle. Gravity was as much a 'Ghost in the Machine' of a physical description of the universe as was the mind in the description of persons – but it has been a long time since anyone doubted the existence of gravity!

---

## Uncertainty and microtubes – a way out?

Just as Cartesian mechanics gave way to Newtonian physics, that too has given way to relativity and quantum mechanics and it is therefore tempting (but probably, in the long run, unproductive) to look to the new physics for some way out of the freedom/ determinism problem.

Quantum theory shows that, at the sub-atomic level, there is fundamental uncertainty; everything remains in a wave form, with its precise location indeterminate, until observed. Once observed, the wave collapses into some definite state or other. Thus you have an element of freedom and randomness, in place of the older Newtonian physics of fixed physical laws. Is it possible that consciousness resides in some such level within the brain, below the level of neurones?

It has been observed that all living cells have protein structures made up of microtubes and that these microtubes may be related to what we know as consciousness. Like the sub-atomic particles, they may be indeterminate until accessed. If so, freedom creeps in at the bottom rung of the physical ladder. But that hardly does justice to the experience of freedom operating at the level of the whole complex entity.

It is also true that even strictly deductive systems, like mathematics, cannot ever prove all their basic assumptions. There comes a point at which the explanation of fundamental principles remains incomplete, complete proof is impossible – this was put forward by Kurt Gödel and is generally referred to as Gödel's theorem.

---

### COMMENT

Since quantum mechanics has shown fundamental indeterminism, shattering the certainties of the older Newtonian physics, and since Gödel has shown that not even mathematics can sort out its own foundations completely, it is tempting to see both areas as opening the way for a kind of indeterminacy that will allow mental activity to have an impact on the physical world.

In practice, however, this is not very helpful. The quantum theorist Erwin Schrödinger (famous for his 'Schrödinger's Cat' thought experiment) pointed out that quantum indeterminacy operates only at the sub-atomic level. At the level of human beings, the quantum approach is simply not appropriate.

Just because mathematics is not totally self-justifying or the sub-atomic particles are not predictable does not stop $2 + 2 = 4$ from remaining true or challenge the speed of acceleration of a ball rolling down a slope. Thus we may indeed find that there is quantum indeterminacy in microtubes, but that is not necessarily relevant at the level of individual mental activity and its resulting physical action.

## Freedom as an Illusion

Spinoza took the view that everything in the world was totally determined by physical causes (see page 24), and that there was therefore no scope for human freedom. And this, of course, has been the approach of materialists and behaviourists, who have also tried to fit the idea of mind into a closed system of physical cause and effect.

But if this is the case, why is it that we have the illusion of freedom? How can I so easily be fooled into thinking that I have choice or that I make a difference as I type these words into my computer? Why do I sense that I am responsible for what I do?

Spinoza's answer is that we simply do not understand all the complex sets of causes that determine what happens. Now, this is clear enough. We know some causes and physical limitations. If I sense that I am launching myself from a window and gently floating on the wind, I know that I am dreaming, for unaided flight is a physical impossibility for human beings. But I have to accept that I do not know *all* the possible influences on my actions. Thus, for example, my therapist would be quick to point out causes of my actions of which I was quite unaware. Many influences from my past, long forgotten, may shape my present action.

The approach taken by Spinoza is therefore reasonable as far as it goes. If I knew absolutely everything there is to know, then I would know that there are very good reasons for every apparently 'free' decision I make. The fact that I can be indecisive or that I think I am making a completely free choice, simply reflects my ignorance.

---

**COMMENT**

Notice the presupposition of this approach: that there is a single set of causes, of which we assume our freedom to act is one and that complete knowledge of all the other causes shows that there is no 'gap' within which freedom can insert its own particular causal input. By contrast, my experience of freedom is not that of finding a gap in which to make a difference, but acting as an agent in and through the many other laws and principles that govern physical life. I do not deny, when steering my car to the right, that there is a complete explanation for that action – from the steering mechanism and tyre grip on the road, through to the activity in my brain. Rather, that whole physical system is doing what it is doing *because* I am choosing to turn right.

# The experience of freedom

Kant argued that there was a fundamental difference between things as we experience them (*phenomena*) and things as they are in themselves (*noumena*). When I examine anything in the world, I do so in terms of categories of thought, including space, time and causality. Every object is determined by these categories, because that is the way our minds deal with objects. We do not see objects (including observed human objects) as free agents, but look to see what has caused them to act.

By the same token, I experience my own freedom. I do so, not as an 'object' of someone else's experience, but as a 'noumenal' subject. If I tried to look at myself as an object, as I might do if being asked to explain the course of my career, for example, then I would try to explain the influences upon me. If radically honest, I would present myself as an object. But that would not be the way I had actually lived my life; each choice along the way would have expressed my own experience of freedom.

Kant's argument is that we are, at one and the same time, phenomenally conditioned and noumenally free.

**COMMENT**

This view has the advantage of seeing freedom as something that is experienced through actions that, to someone else, would appear to be causally conditioned. I do not need to find a 'gap' within which freedom can operate – it operates throughout.

## Morality

Are we morally responsible? If freedom is an illusion and if everything is physically determined, we have no choice in our actions. In that case, it makes little sense to say that actions are morally significant. If I cannot influence my actions, they cannot be deemed either good or bad.

In order for anything to be a moral issue, the person concerned has to be exactly that – a 'person'. Machines are not morally responsible, only those who design, manufacture or use them. No gun has ever been guilty of murder, only the person pulling the trigger.

If morality depends only on the performance of an action and intentions are left out of the consideration, then goodness and badness are determined by society and may be applied in any circumstances. If the person concerned argues that he is actually an automaton, totally determined within an overall system (perhaps along the lines of Spinoza's argument set out earlier), then there is no question of guilt about what has happened. Contrariwise, the judge passing sentence could argue that the punishment is equally determined and that he is not free to offer clemency.

Once the intention of the person becomes significant and morality becomes a matter of following personally held principles – even to the point of going against society and its rules in order to hold to a more general or deeply held view or commitment – then it is clear that moral praise or blame must assume that the subject is an *autonomous individual*.

There can be pressure, extenuating circumstances and so on, but, ultimately, you have to believe that, for praise or blame, there is a person who sees a situation and responds freely to it, doing what he or she wishes, therefore reflecting his or her desires, values and intentions. Morality, without individuals who experience themselves as free to choose, makes no sense.

The point here is that, from a scientific (including a psychological) point of view, everything can be phenomenologically determined. Every lawbreaker has a reason to break the law and that reason may be to do with upbringing, values, circumstances and so on. If an action is not completely random (and banks do not get robbed by random passers-by!), there are reasons for its having taken place.

That said, for those taking part in the game of life, there are choices to be made, choices that lead to moral praise or blame. The experience is of freedom and with it comes guilt or self-satisfaction, moral praise or blame. Of course, as Heidegger pointed out (see page 77) I am 'thrown' into my situation in life and can never know the totality of the background influences upon me, but that does not stop me from affirming myself. To give way on the issue of human freedom is to abdicate what is distinctive about being human; to choose to see oneself as an 'object' rather than affirming oneself as a 'subject'.

# Actions, intentions and beliefs

We do what we do because of our beliefs. If I am thirsty and believe that there is a beer in the fridge, I will go over and open the fridge door. The belief (about the beer) leads to the action – in other words there is a 'predictive strategy' based on that belief. The belief is real enough and can presumably be identified with a certain pattern of brain behaviour, but it is only known because of the *intentional* nature of conscious behaviour. (For intentionality, see also page 82.)

But the implication of an intentionalist stance is that mind plays an *instrumental* role in human life. In other words, it is known through what it does. Here is Friedrich Nietzsche on the mind:

> What the sense feels, what the spirit perceives, is never an end in itself. But sense and spirit would like to persuade you that they are the end of all things: they are as vain as that.
>
> *Sense and spirit are instruments and toys: behind them still lies the Self* [my emphasis]. The Self seeks with the eyes of the senses; it listens too with the ears of the spirit.
>
> Behind your thoughts and feelings, my brother, stands a mighty commander, an unknown sage – he is called Self. He lives in your body, he is your body... Your Self laughs at your Ego and its proud leapings. 'What are these leapings and flights of thought to me?' it says to itself. 'A by-way to my goal. I am the Ego's leading-string and I prompt its conceptions.'

The Self says to the Ego: 'Feel pain!' Thereupon it suffers
and gives thought how to end its suffering – and it is *meant*
to think for just that purpose.

*(Thus Spake Zarathustra)*

Thus, for Nietzsche, the self is not the same as consciousness, but
is more physical – the living body. Whereas we may think that
consciousness is an end in itself, as the final goal in the quest for
who we are, Nietzsche shatters this by showing that these have a
function to perform, they are instruments that serve to achieve
some end, an end determined by the self.

---

**IN OTHER WORDS**

Actions are an expression of the self. The self controls feelings
and thoughts; they are vehicles for getting things done, not ends
in themselves. The self is that which acts and has goals, which
seeks to develop itself and move forward. This is what it means
to be a conscious, living being. In the case of humankind, of
course, the self can call upon a rich array of mental and
emotional tools with which to express itself and forward its aims
in life.

I sense that, if Nietzsche were asked if we were free to act
(following some discussion of the problem of freedom and
determinism), he would probably say that action is determined
by the self, with both body and mind as mere instruments.

Is freedom possible then? Only for those who have the courage
of their convictions!

# 8 | CONSCIOUSNESS

What does it mean to be conscious? How do I know that someone else is conscious? How is consciousness related to what is going on in the brain? Is disembodied consciousness possible?

It is one of the very worst features of philosophy that it can sometimes delight in making the obvious seem improbable. There have been many arguments outlined in this book that might suggest that consciousness does not really exist or is really no more than a disposition to behave in a certain way. However, we know what it is to be conscious and to say that someone is conscious – in other words, we have an intuitive knowledge of consciousness. What is difficult is actually defining and explaining it.

Probably as good a starting point as any is to distinguish between simple consciousness and *reflective self-consciousness*. The latter is a human quality of being not only aware, but aware that one is aware: it allows a person to reflect, rather than just accept, his or her experiences and responses to them. But consciousness itself operates also at a simpler, unreflective level. Consciousness is an awareness of the external world; it is the subjective aspect of what it means to sense and respond to something.

In other words, it would seem inappropriate to say that the eye or the optic nerve was conscious, but if, as a result of the operation of the eye and the optic nerve, you can see and be aware of things around you, then *you* can be said to be conscious. Consciousness does not reside in the sense organs themselves, but is used to describe what is happening when the sense organs are transmitting information which is being processed and to which a response can be given.

You do not need to give much of a physical response – after all, you could be conscious but paralysed. However, to lose consciousness is to stop showing any response to stimulus. Indeed, going unconscious is one of the body's defence mechanisms against unbearable pain.

---

### Qualia

Qualia is the term used for the basic 'phenomenal qualities' of experience – the taste of something, its colour or texture, the sound of a piece of music. In many ways they are the building blocks of mental life – the simplest elements of experience. However, it is very difficult to explain qualia, except in terms of other qualia or subjective experience as a whole. Why should it be that photons entering the eyeball cause me to see this particular thing? What is the relationship between the information reaching my brain and the experience of seeing?

Qualia cause a problem for the functionalist approach to mind. If the mind is simply a processor that receives inputs and decides the appropriate responses (which is, crudely put, what functionalism claims) then how do we account for this whole 'qualia' level of conscious experience? Qualia do not appear as a function, but neither are they physical.

---

So let us start with a view that is not just common sense, but also, quite simply, true – we all know what consciousness is, both as we experience it in ourselves and when we encounter it in others. We recognise it, even if we find it hard to define. Thus for example, I know that a dog is conscious but that a stone is not. I can imagine what it might be like to be a dog, to see and respond to pleasure by wagging my tail! I have at least some idea, by analogy with my own, of what it might be like to have a dog's consciousness. Contrariwise, I cannot imagine what it would be like to be a stone, to be solid and inert, without inwardness of any sort. Consciousness is obvious; it is not the end point of a journey of discovery, but its starting point.

### Example

While writing this book I had the sad duty of burying a family pet, my daughter's dog Sykes. Usually, on approaching the house, Sykes would come to greet me, wagging her tail in recognition. I would get licked all over. I only had to touch a lead and Sykes knew that it was time to go for a walk. She would respond to human language, sometimes turning her head to indicate that she hadn't quite understood what was said, but was interested. A familiar word would elicit an immediate response. Many photos show her curled up with my daughter, giving and receiving affection. Sykes was definitely conscious.

But this time, the familiar animal lay still on her bedding. No heartbeat, no brain activity, muscles slack; otherwise she looked fine. But, beyond the physical description, notice what is lacking – there is no response, no interaction with the world around her.

The missing element is consciousness and that would have been equally true were she in a coma rather than dead. It is impossible not to know in oneself and to recognise in others – human or animal – that essential ingredient that is consciousness.

Therefore, even though difficult to define, consciousness is easily recognised. I may be conscious of a pleasure or a pain – in other words, I am aware of it. Thus, one aspect of consciousness concerns the processing of information that comes through the senses. But consciousness cannot be limited to experiencing and responding (remember Searle's 'Chinese Room' problem – see page 77). We may be conscious of having (or having had) a dream. That dream is certainly something that happens in our consciousness and may be very significant for us, but it is not related to sense experiences. One may also be conscious of not receiving external stimuli – I may be conscious of feeling nothing or seeing nothing – nevertheless, I am still conscious. Perhaps, with apologies to Descartes, one might say that 'I am conscious, therefore I am'. In other words, consciousness is what takes place where there is any sentient awareness, whether that awareness is of something internally generated or of external stimuli. Consciousness concerns that subjective quality of experience – in other words (as defined earlier) its qualia.

**Note**

'Computational neuroscience' is the term used for the examination of the way electro-chemical signals are used by the brain to represent and process information. Since the brain is a huge parallel processor, it should not be assumed that bits of information are stored sequentially or at the same level of complexity. It is likely that many things are produced by higher order organisational patterns, which involve groups of neurones from different areas of the brain.

Consciousness may be seen either as *a feature that emerges in a complex and multi-layered reality* – not an alternative to physical reality, but an aspect of that reality once a certain level of complexity has been reached – or as *a fundamental feature of the world itself, irreducible to physical processes.*

David Chalmers, in the opening of his book *The Conscious Mind* (1996), makes the point that consciousness is a natural phenomenon and that it should therefore be capable of scientific explanation, even if we cannot give one at the moment. But that, of course, does not mean that consciousness can be reduced in a materialist way. His view is that consciousness arises from the organisation of what is going on in the brain and is therefore not seen if it is simply reduced to brain activity itself.

**Brain features and mind features**

John Searle (in *Minds, Brains and Computers*) makes the absolutely crucial point that, although brain activity may cause mental activity, and mental operations may therefore reflect what is happening in the brain, that does not mean that the way of describing the two things will be the same or that one makes the other redundant. He gives the example of the desk at which he writes being hard and knows that it relates to the lattice structure of the molecules of which it is make. Similarly, the wetness of water is a feature of water molecules. But that does not mean that hardness and wetness are features of something *other than* those molecules. It makes no sense at all to say that a water molecule is wet – since wetness does not show up at the molecular level. But at the same time, what is wet is nothing other than the liquid made up of molecules.

Thus, in exploring consciousness, we are dealing with features that are quite different from patterns of neurones firing in the brain. But that does not mean that they are not real neither does it mean that they do not refer to those neurones and to nothing other than them.

What we can say with some degree of certainty is that the neurophysiology of the brain is intimately linked with what we experience as the mental process. Brain function both *causes* and *realises* mental states. We are not going to find some 'other' place where mind is located, but equally, it would be a reductionist folly to try to *identify* brain with mind. Mental states – thoughts, hopes, ideas, wants, regrets – may be the experience that takes place alongside particular patterns of neurophysiological activity, but they are also related to past experiences and to the broad area of shared consciousness that constitutes human culture.

**COMMENT**

What happens in our mind can no more be the product of a single brain than the information on the Internet can be the product of a single computer memory. When the mind thinks, it is more like 'logging on' than simply 'turning on'. Words, concepts, values, relationships and our overall situation in life – all these things inform our mental activity. But they are not our personal property. We are an efficient receptor of the thoughts that form the common experience of humankind.

# Disembodied consciousness

Before looking at whether or not consciousness can exist without a body, we need to return for a moment and consider exactly what it is we mean by consciousness. If we take it to refer to the whole range of mental activities, covering both the awareness a creature has of its environment and its response to it, then it is difficult to see how it can be disembodied, since consciousness must surely include sensation. But is sensation a mental function or is it related to the body? We know that, while asleep, we may believe that we are receiving sensations that are not actually taking place. Does that put sensations into a separate category from other mental activities, such that deprived of sensations (which clearly must be the case if a mind is disembodied) consciousness can carry on.

One thinker who was very clear about the role of sensations was John Stuart Mill. In *The System of Logic* (1872) he categorised mental phenomena as comprising thoughts, emotions, volitions *and* sensations. Of the latter he said:

> As truly states of Mind as the three former. It is usual, indeed, to speak of sensations as states of body, not of mind. But this is the common confusion of giving one and the same name to a phenomenon and to the proximate cause or conditions of the phenomenon. The immediate antecedent of a sensation is a state of body, but the sensation itself is a state of mind. If the word mind means anything, it means that which feels.

Thus the external world and the bodily means of getting in touch with that world are physical, but the sensations themselves are mental. As we have seen earlier, there is always the possibility of confusion, because we speak of seeing 'a red shape', for example, and mean there exists something red in the physical world external to our body. But we have also seen that 'a red shape' only makes sense in terms of our mental process of sensation. What is 'out there' may produce light of a particular frequency and this may be translated into nerve impulses and so on — but the actual experience of 'a red shape' is what happens when that information is received by the mind and becomes a sensation.

The issue here is no different from that which separates materialists, dualists, functionalists and so on. It is the basic problem of how the physical and mental are related and where the demarcation between the two is drawn.

But the crucial question for us here is this: If sensations are mental events and yet are caused directly by the bodily reception of stimuli from the external physical world, how is it possible for a 'mind' to exist in a disembodied state?

One possibility here is that of someone asleep or (more significantly) in a deep coma. In these situations one may say that the mind is still active and yet there are clearly no further sensory inputs. Hence there can be thoughts, emotions and volitions in the complete absence of sensations.

But how can we know? One possibility would be to study brain activity during sleep or of a comatose patient. But what does this show? It shows a physical, not a mental phenomenon — for brain activity, like the sensory nerves that transmit information to the brain, is clearly on the physical side of the physical/mental divide. The possibility of disembodied mental activity is only known because, on returning to consciousness, a person claims to have had that activity – in the form of dreams. There are two issues of particular interest here, the possibility of life after death and 'out of body' experiences.

## Life after death

This is a contradiction in terms, which nevertheless takes on particular significance emotionally and for religious views of the nature of reality and human destiny.

The issue is clear. For all but those taking a strictly materialist view, mental phenomena are not identified with physical activity (including brain activity). Hence, it may be argued that they might exist in the absence of any physical activity.

The problem, however, is that there is no knowledge of mental activity other than through the mediation of physical activity. I may remember that I had a dream last night, but that act of remembering (although not *what* I remember) may be detected as brain activity. What is more, any act of reporting mental activity is physical. Even if it is thought that one might receive information from another person by telepathy, that cannot be known unless expressed and it cannot be expressed without a body to do the expressing.

Hence, even if it were possible to speculate about a dream-like state in which mental activity took place, one would need to ask how this would make any sense without physical activity in the brain and how one could ever show that it had taken place.

In other words, that which is not physically detectable and cannot be reported without involving physical activity cannot be known.

Of course, from the religious point of view, life after death is linked to issues of great personal significance:

■ It offers a sense of appropriate compensation, good or bad, for what a person has done or experienced during his or her life. Religious traditions generally have some element of reward or punishment beyond death for deeds done in this life, whether that is externally imposed (as in western religions) or self-generated (as in the 'karma' of eastern traditions). But surely, what such beliefs are emphasising is the transcendent nature of the mind; that a person's life has significance that goes beyond the limited fortunes of the physical body. The desire for reward or punishment is a desire that the true value of the human person should be acknowledged in a way that cannot be the case in terms of a limited physical life.

■ It also expresses the sense that human life somehow goes 'beyond' the confines of a fragile human body – the sense that there must be something more to life than one is capable of experiencing here and now.

Neither of these constitutes *evidence* for survival of death. What they do show is the *appropriateness* of such belief for a religious person and the reasons why he or she might hold to it in the absence of evidence.

## Near-death experiences

About one-third of all those who have given accounts of having been very close to death (or pronounced dead, even) and have subsequently recovered, describe what are termed 'near-death experiences'. As a phenomenon, it is neither rare nor limited to people with any particular set of religious beliefs.

Typical of such an experience is an awareness of the self, floating above the operating table on which one's now nearly dead body is lying and looking down at the scene. It is generally accompanied by a sense of well being, detachment from the traumas of the body and sometimes of relief and happy anticipation. There are frequent descriptions of moving down through a dark tunnel towards some comforting light at the end. Then there is generally a sense that one has to go back, of being physically drawn down into the body again, sometimes almost with a sense of regret.

One theory is that such experiences are brought about because the brain is starved of oxygen and that a 'near-death experience' is actually simply the qualia associated with brain states that occur as the brain itself is 'shutting down' (to use a computer analogy). If so, it simply confirms the linking of qualia and brain states, those in the final stages of the life of a brain being reported only by those who survive such situations.

## An existentialist view

Heidegger explored the nature of what he termed *Dasein*, what it is for humans 'to be'. In other words, he was looking at the nature and purpose of 'being', seen particularly from a human standpoint. He recognised that there are many facts that determine who we are – facts about the world into which, in his terms, we are 'thrown'. We cannot escape from the thrownness of our nature any more than we can escape from the fact of death – that our life is finite. What we can do, according to Heidegger, is make choices that reflect our personal aims in life, rather than simply conform to what others or the situation expects of us. This is what it means to live in an 'authentic' rather than an 'inauthentic' way.

Now, Heidegger's thought is complex and his style and language is far from easy to cope with, but (particularly in his principal work, *Being and Time*) he showed how the experience of human life was related to the fundamental issues of being, and that it was lived in all three time zones, with the present always influenced by the thrownness of the past, but also the goals and aspirations that we look for in the future.

The key feature of his thought (and that of existentialism in general), for the purpose of the philosophy of mind, is to recognise that existential questions are very different from ontological ones. Most philosophers start by asking if the self exist, and what it can be like. Existential thinkers, however, do not ask 'if' the self exists but rather look at what the self is doing and how it relates to the structures of existence. In other words, for existentialist philosophy, the self plays a formative role, shaping itself by its decisions, always relating to other people and the rest of the world. The self is thus a function, or process; it is not a fixed entity. To behave in an authentic way is to express the reality of self in the light of the reality of the world, it is to affirm one's freedom to choose. To deny this is to retreat back into the idea that everything is determined by outside influences (the 'they' for Heidegger) and the thrownness of our origins, whereas the true vocation of humanity is to live in a way that is authentic and free from external constraints, following our goals by making concrete decisions about what we are to do with life.

Jean-Paul Sartre (1905–1980) argued that consciousness was always consciousness 'of' something and that consciousness was therefore not an entity in itself. Consciousness is related to everything that is not itself. In this sense, consciousness is a 'total emptiness'.

---

**IN OTHER WORDS**

The attempt to look at our own consciousness requires us to see it as a 'thing' – but then it automatically becomes *part of* the world of which we are conscious. In other words, we are trying to make an object out of subjectivity, which is impossible. Consciousness is like an eye that sees everything except itself; therefore Sartre can describe consciousness as a 'nonsubstantial absolute'.

In many ways, this is like Wittgenstein's saying that the self is not *part* of the world, but rather the *boundary* of the world.

---

There is another important element to the existentialist approach. Sartre makes the distinction between 'being in itself' and 'being for itself'. The latter is the personal subject, aware of itself in its relationships with the external world. 'Being in itself', by way of contrast, is being insofar as it is a fixed 'object', something which just 'is' but which does not ask existential questions.

To see the self as 'being in itself' is to limit it, to see it simply in terms of how it responds to external influences, to reduce it to a thing that can be observed and shaped. It is rather like Heidegger's 'inauthentic' self that only responds to the bidding of external forces.

'Being for itself' is an active agent, defining and shaping itself through choices made as a result of its contact with the world.

Clearly, consciousness is to do with 'being for itself'; but the problem of looking at consciousness is that there is a tendency to objectivise it, to show where it 'fits in' – in other words, to make it 'being in itself'. Analysed in this way, it is no surprise that consciousness vanishes.

---

**IN OTHER WORDS**

For existential thinkers, the self is what gives meaning and significance to life, choosing the future and responding to influences from the past. It can do so precisely to the extent that it does *not* allow itself to be objectivised or put within a causal structure that denies its very essence.

# **9** | **THE CREATIVE MIND**

## Too narrow a view?

One of the problems for philosophers who consider questions of minds, bodies and consciousness is that their own experience of the mental life may be too narrowly focused. Those who spend their lives teaching and examining students tend to see mental activity as heavily dependent on the ability to process information and respond to questions, to articulate them in terms of language and to investigate and categorise experience. After all, that is the stuff of life for an academic.

Now, with that approach to mind, it is reasonable to take a view of artificial intelligence that hopes to create a mind rather like a perfect student, logical sequences and information being programmed and accessed when required.

In actual fact, the mind is perhaps better appreciated by the existentialists or those concerned with the creative arts. The processing of information is part – but only part – of what the brain does and it is certainly not the whole of what it means to be a human being.

Processing depends on pre-established goals. I know if a computer works well, because I expect it to perform certain tasks – as stated on the box the software came in. I measure performance against the accomplishment of those tasks and hence the delivery of the goals I require. Part of the problem with using a computer as an analogy for the human process of thinking and consciousness is that it denies the essential element of freedom that characterises human life. The office worker who assesses his or her life simply on performance across a desk is judged a sad character! The key feature of human consciousness is that it constantly breaks out of the moulds into which others try to fit it.

People only settle into a narrow view of their life's potential out of fear of the scope of their consciousness and where it might lead them. The existential philosopher, therapist, novelist or playwright is likely to have a better notion of what human consciousness is about than the philosopher studying the possibility of creating artificial intelligence. To someone who attempted to programme a computer to compose a Beethoven symphony, in the desperate attempt to understand Beethoven, I would say: 'If you want to understand Beethoven, don't try to reproduce him artificially, go out and listen to (or better, perform in) one of his symphonies!'

Analysis and reconstruction may be useful if one is trying to understand the workings of a crude mechanical device, but it really doesn't work with human consciousness! It assumes far too narrow a view of what the human mind is about.

Perhaps one of the clues to understanding human minds and their workings is to remember to look at those things that are of an appropriate size. If dealing with humans, it is little use remaining focused on the microscopic workings of neurones.

---

### Size matters!

If too close a focus on the processing of information as a sign of intelligent life is a problem, so is the issue of size and complexity. Human beings are extremely complex creatures and it is important to recognise that their 'selfhood' operates at the holistic level. If you attempt a physical analysis of the brain in order to locate mental operations you cannot get to the heart of the experience of consciousness – for the neurones are just too small to give a picture of the life of the whole person.

What about all the bacteria that inhabit my mouth and gut? They perform a valuable task in digesting food and so on. But are they part of *me*? Taken at the microscopic level there is much that is happening within my skin to which I pay no attention and which, as an individual, I regard as irrelevant. Cells reproduce themselves with no conscious interference on my part. Much of what we are carries on regardless. To what extent is all that microscopic activity 'me'? Is the 'real me' not primarily visible at the point at which I make conscious decisions?

And then there is the matter of social interaction. We do not inhabit a world devoid of other human beings. If we did, most of what makes us an individual would be taken away. We are social creatures, dependent at every moment on the environment that supports us. Isolated from that environment, our life expectancy is scarcely a couple of minutes – however long we can survive without drawing breath.

There is a real sense in which the question 'Who am I?' has to be answered in terms of different levels. Only within a fairly narrow band of size and complexity will the individual appear. Taken to the microscopic level, I vanish in the hectic activity of millions of individual cells. Taken to the macrocosmic, the human species is little more than an interconnecting network of fine dust grains, spread across the thin film of biosphere, on a tiny planet. Only at the level in which my whole self can perceive and respond to other creatures at that same level can we start to have what we call mental life. Only in terms of those relationships do I start to become a self.

On the cosmic scale, our galaxy is eating a small neighbour, but that does not concern us enough to put us off eating our own lunch. And once we have done so, even with the best of dental hygiene, the bacteria in our mouth will start to have their lunch. Every meal is three meals in one – but only the middle one, of which we are immediately conscious, is significant for considering the nature of our own life.

Let us be clear about the implications of size for our understanding of mind. Of course, I am host to millions of microbes, all living out their lives within my body. Of course, at every moment, there are cells reproducing, white blood cells cruising around looking for foreign invaders to eat, cells growing and then being told by the body to kill themselves because they are in the wrong place. I am a universe of activity, but most of it is of no direct concern to me.

However, if some of those cells start reproducing wrongly, I am in serious trouble. If a microscopic virus gains a foothold in my body, I will get ill. The different physical levels are therefore far from independent of one another. I cannot exist without all those cells and their activity. But my sentient life – my mind and consciousness – operates only at a holistic level, at which I, as a human being, relate to others, explore my own hopes and fears and so on.

Equally, the atoms of which I am composed were created billions of years ago. The same substances of which I am composed are found throughout the universe – I am part of that greater reality. I know that the present universe will change; stars come and go, taking planets with them. Galaxies collide. The conditions that enable human beings to survive are very precise and temporary. We are here for a very short time on the surface of this planet, a lucky chance in an inhospitable universe.

But, again, that does not generally concern me. My mind does not operate at the universal level, but at the human. True, a stray chunk of cosmic debris could wipe out life on earth, but that is so beyond my ability to intervene and do anything about it, that I do not take it into consideration.

If we are to consider the nature of mind, it must be at the level at which mind works and that is neither the cosmic nor the microscopic, but the personal and individual.

# Religion and metaphysics

In the mediaeval world, fear of eternal damnation and the fate of the soul after death were great religious motivators. That has largely gone, but we might still ask about the broad religious and metaphysical implications of the study of the mind. If the mind really is creative, what does it say about religion or the idea of a life beyond the limits of the physical body?

There are philosophers who give to mind a supremely creative function. One of the most challenging features of the philosophy of Friedrich Nietzsche is his argument that we are called on to shape and mould our own lives very much in the way that an artist sets about creating an image. If he is right, then we are our own creators, that we have ultimate responsibility for the direction of our lives. He saw that as necessary, if we are to have any sense of purpose in a world in which God was dead.

Now, whether or not one agrees with Nietzsche – and the debate about the death of God is far beyond our present concern – it is clear that one can see the creative function of mind as absolutely central to an understanding of the world as a whole (in other words, metaphysics).

This view is by no means new. A key feature of the philosophy of the Buddha in the 6th century BCE is that our life is the creation of our mind and that every thought we have and every choice we make has a part to play in shaping our future. To understand my present situation, I have to look at my thoughts and choices of yesterday. To know my future, I have to examine my present thoughts and choices. Rather than considering the mind to be some esoteric entity whose relationship to the material world is problematic, the Buddha starts with the experienced reality of mental activity. Our minds are what solve our problems and decide what we should do – they are the shaping force that directs the material body.

From such a Nietzschian or Buddhist perspective, it is nonsense to try grubbing about among the neurones for the seat of consciousness. The mind is that which, through a constant process of exploring, learning and responding, relates the individual to his or her environment and takes charge of the many functions that are necessary for life, from controlling breathing, feeling sexually aroused and able to reproduce, seeking out satisfaction for hunger, thirst, devising means of avoiding excessive heat and cold — and on through the whole complex process of modern human society.

## Beyond death?

We have already touched on ideas of life after death and near-death experiences, but a consideration of the creative nature of mind raises the question as to whether it has a role in seeing the significance of the individual in a way that is not physically limited. The idea of a life that transcends death, either by continuing afterwards in some way or by belonging to a different realm (the eternal) which is not touched by the changes and final ending of the physical body is held by a majority of religious people of all world faiths.

Clearly, of the various possibilities in terms of the relationship between the self and the physical body, survival of any sort requires dualism. If the self is not both separate from the body and capable of surviving without the continuing presence of the body (as in epiphenomenal approaches – see page 22) then it makes no sense to speak of a self continuing after death or separate from the physical body.

What is the 'beyond' we are concerned with here? First of all, in a spacetime continuum, time and space are linked; if something is eternal, it must be beyond any limitations of time and therefore also beyond any limitations of space. In other words, it is logically impossible (given the nature of the universe we live in) to have something which is physically limited and located, but also eternal. If eternal life means anything, it is about the role of the self physically beyond the individual body.

That being the case, one might look on the expanding identities of the self and the way this relates to the eventual dissolution of its physical matrix:

- As far as the individual goes, death of the physical body is certain.
- For a family or organisation, the physical reality goes beyond any one individual.
- For a larger group, such as a nation or race, life continues through others who share that nationality or racial group.
- For humanity, continuity is more realistic, being limited only by the conditions that prevail on earth being compatible with human existence.
- One might go further (as in Buddhism and Jainism) and contemplate unity within all sentient life.
- Finally, one can have some sort of identity with the universe as a whole.

Clearly, the life of the self is proportional to the dimensions of the physical reality *with which it is identified*. If the focus is on the human individual, it is always going to prove difficult to argue for a personal and natural immortality, simply because the physical matrix that gives the individual identity is temporary.

Only by extending the concept of 'self' *outwards* to include a wider and wider physical matrix does the extension of the life of that self become more realistic.

### Example

A war hero, deliberately sacrificing himself in the heat of battle, sees himself at that moment as simply part of a larger group – that of his nation. His or her life means something, continues even, through that wider identification. The same would apply to a religious martyr or those who sacrifice themselves to save friends or family.

*Your life is what you identify as your life.* If your life is simply what goes on in and around your body, with the wider world there solely to provide what you need – then you are inevitably doomed. Your physical focus is certainly going to end your life in a decisive way. Those who say 'my family is my life' already acknowledge a sense of life beyond their own death.

And so on – until the mystic, who is able in some way to identify his or her life with the universe as a whole, loses all fear of death. The ending of the body is almost irrelevant, for 'life' (in the sense of what one 'is') has expanded outwards to embrace everything.

### COMMENT

*The creative mind thus creates its own experience of immortality. It cannot simply 'continue', just as it is, onwards through time – for that would require a permanent but limited physical existence. Rather, it can expand its awareness outwards; creating a sense of self that is progressively freed from its physical origins.*

# The creative arts

Artistic creativity is a fact of human life and culture and has been since the earliest cave paintings. It is, of course, closely linked with religious sensitivity – since both religion and the arts seek to express the meaning and significance of life.

In terms of the philosophy of mind, creativity goes against any sense that the mind is a mere epiphenomenon, produced as an accidental and impotent offshoot of brain activity. However intimately it is linked with what happens in the brain, artistic creativity certainly goes beyond any mechanical or predetermined processing of experience. The artist 'sees as' in a variety of ways and the experience of a work of art can change one's own ways of perception.

The process of musical composition, for example, is one that allows emotions to be encapsulated in a physical form quite unlike that within which the emotions were originally encountered, but which is able to ignite those emotions in others. The love of the countryside is not, in itself, a musical experience. Yet there is music that can evoke a sense of rural bliss. Similarly with war, patriotism or tragic loss. Those emotions and experiences are handled and processed (consciously or unconsciously) by the composer, so that they may be evoked in the hearer.

There is, of course, debate between modernism and postmodernism on the role of the creative artist or author. All we need to do here is to be aware that, whether expressing a personal essence or gathering together bits of preformed cultural material, there is a creative role that enables the self to shape and give meaning to physical entities. What the artist produces (like it or hate it) is said to 'mean something' to the artist or to be a statement about how that artist sees reality.

---

**IN OTHER WORDS**

The artistic self is not passive, but active. It does not simply register and respond to external reality, but creates. Any view of the self that does not take artistic creativity into account is inadequate.

# A Buddhist perspective

Buddhist philosophy is particularly concerned to explore the nature of the self, since it argues that a limited and fixed idea of self is the root cause of suffering. Indeed, breaking down conventional notions of the self is central to the Buddhist path.

Buddhist philosophy is complex and reflects the many different cultural traditions embraced by the Buddhist tradition. Nevertheless, there are some basic views of the nature of the self that are part of the earliest tradition and therefore reflect the approach of a majority of Buddhist thinkers.

Key to Buddhist thinking is the idea that the 'self' is merely a conventional idea and that ultimately there is no fixed or permanent self. What we know as the self is, in fact, 'put together' from many parts. The popular Buddhist analogy is with the chariot, which cannot be identified with the axle, wheels or any other part of which it is made and yet does not exist other than as the assembly of those parts.

The Buddha suggested that a person is made up of five '*skandhas*' (or bundles), namely:

- Form – our physical body, including its sense organs; this is seen as constantly changing and completely dependent on its material environment.
- Sensations – including all sense impressions, also ideas, for the Buddha regarded the mind as a form of sixth sense, gathering and registering ideas.
- Perceptions – the mind can only understand the sensations it receives by a process of conceptualisation. Perceptions are the 'seeing as' of western thought.
- Mental formations – these are the habitual attitudes and actions that are our response to our sensations and perceptions. They give us our character.
- Consciousness – this is the fundamental awareness of being alive and processing all that comes to us through the senses. Each sense is said to have its own distinctive form of consciousness.

The Buddha's view was that each of these five *skandhas* is constantly changing. Nothing is fixed. There is no separate, permanent, eternal 'soul' or self (a teaching known as *anatta*). Buddhism is not a speculative philosophy as much as a programme of personal development, with a view to increasing wisdom and compassion. Each teaching therefore has a particular, existential purpose in mind and practical consequences.

The teaching of *anatta* is designed to avoid the suffering that comes from craving and the roots of craving are seen in the false notion that we are permanent and fixed and that the rest of the world is somehow there to provide for us.

The recognition that the self is a flow of experiences, coming into being and passing away in response to circumstances is seen as a more realistic view of the reality of life, and therefore as a basis for seeing common cause with all other sentient beings.

---

**COMMENT**

It is very difficult to fit the Buddhist view of the self into any of the western categories. It is certainly not dualistic in a Cartesian sense, neither does it see the mind (or self – since the thinking 'mind', for Buddhist philosophy, is almost like an extra sense, over and above sensations, volitions and so on) as merely a by-product of physical activity. Rather, both physical and mental realms are in a state of flux, with entities being distorted as soon as they are fixed conceptually. In other words, as soon as I start to clarify 'my mind' or 'my body' I am already moving away from the ever-changing reality, towards a distorted and distorting notion of permanence.

---

For our purpose, it is enough to note that, from a Buddhist perspective, the notion of the self is the key to all else – on the grounds that one cannot understand the nature of the world or know how to respond to it positively without a realistic view of the self.

This is very different from Western religion and philosophy, which has tended to start with overall speculation about the nature of things (metaphysics) or the nature of God and has then developed an idea of the self to fit those existing ideas.

Ironically, it is modern science that has shown the folly of that approach. It recognises that an understanding of the world is always shaped by the ways in which we perceive it: we cannot get a truly 'objective' view of anything.

In other words: we understand the world only by means of our own consciousness. Hence, if we do not appreciate how we look at things, we will never understand the things we are seeing.

## And sometimes I just sit...

Sometimes you can sit and think and at other times you just sit. Part of the curse of the mind/body issue and many of the problems that arise when considering consciousness is the fact that (as Hume said) we never experience ourselves except as having some thought or other. The mind is a continuously running kaleidoscope. But need it be?

One of the most creative experiences, explored in many religions, particularly in the east, but also in many self-help and therapy contexts in the west, is the quieting of the mind in meditation

Naturally, it is difficult to explain meditation experiences, since they contain at best rough analogies with other mental states. But a key feature is the immediacy of experience. The breakthrough comes when we no longer think about what we are doing in meditation, but just enter into the experience itself.

From the moment of meditative absorption the issue 'Who am I?' becomes irrelevant. The very notion of defining the self – and thereby distinguishing the self from everything that is 'not self' – is superficial and pointless.

In many ways (as mystics have claimed from all religious traditions) the self-world distinction can be overcome, we can be aware of ourselves as being part of a universal reality, focused in a particular time and place. Indeed, we can experience the expanding out of the self, so that its particular physical matrix is almost irrelevant.

To be lost in music, enraptured by a work of art, absorbed in a creative activity – all these approach the same experience that is explored through meditation. It is an utter excentration of the self, turning it inside out, so that personal meaning is now experienced as much on the outside as on the inside.

## The cosmic analogy

There was a time when the universe was small, hot, smooth and almost uniform. Only when it started to cool did matter form and hydrogen start to fuse into helium, and then down into the heavier atoms. With the pull of gravity, matter started to separate off and clump together into stars and galaxies. Heavier elements were formed and the universe started to become a far more differentiated place.

And, finally, on planet earth, human beings contemplate the universe and ask how all the various parts relate to one another, whether there might be a theory of everything, what place intelligent life has within such a universe and even whether the universe was programmed to develop in such a way that intelligence was its inevitable product.

And so the mind, product of the cooling and differentiating process of the developing universe, separates itself off from all else and starts asking questions.

And from those questions arise problems and confusion and all the philosophy that we have been exploring in this book.

And yet, whatever mind is, and whatever its physical realisation in the firing of neurones, it is part of a cosmic process. And, in a sense, the moment it lets go of that which differentiates it from all else, it can feel a natural affinity with all that lies around it. It can, in a sense, identify itself with that earlier state, of an undifferentiated universe. It can recognise that its separateness is simply a function of cooling.

To experience that undifferentiated state is not to discover the answers to all the questions we have been setting out in this book, it is to realise that we do not need to ask them.

# GLOSSARY

**behaviourism**   the view that mental attributes apply to physical behaviour.

**cognitive science**   the general term for the range of disciplines which (since the 1970s) work together in considering the nature of human cognition (knowledge).

**consciousness**   a general term with a variety of meanings, including a being's awareness of and response to the environment and also its self-awareness.

**Double Aspect theory**   the view that all reality has both physical and mental aspects.

**dualism**   the view that there are two kinds of substance: physical substance, which has extension and location, and is the object of scientific study, and mental substance, which is not physically located and comprises our thoughts and conscious states. There is also **property dualism** and **concept dualism**, which distinguish mind and body, but without requiring mind to have a separate substance.

**eliminative materialism**   the view that mental phenomena do not exist as such and that a perfect neurobiology would explain all there is to know about the mind.

**epiphenomenalism**   the idea that mind is generated as a result of brain activity, but cannot itself determine brain activity.

**functionalism**   the view that the mind has a functional role in assessing inputs from the senses and giving the appropriate responses. Mental states are not identified with physical states, but the mental does not exist apart from the physical.

**idealism**   the view that there is only one kind of substance, the mental (the physical world we encounter is, in fact, only known in terms of the mental awareness we have of it.)

**intentionality**   the view that all consciousness is directed towards some object and that all thought is therefore 'about' something.

**materialism**   the view that there is only one kind of substance, the physical.

**occasionalism**   the theory that mental sensations occur on the occasion of their corresponding physical occurrences, but are not directly caused by them.

**pre-established harmony**   the view that the mental and physical universes are independent, but designed by God to work together in harmony.

**qualia**   the phenomenological qualities of experience (i.e. the experience of something as having a particular colour, texture, sound).

**solipsism**   the view that we can have no certain knowledge of other minds and are therefore alone in our world.

**structuralism**   an early theory of psychology, which attempted to understand the structure of the mind through the analysis and recording of the phenomena of experience.

**supervenience**   the view that mental properties overlay, rather than replace, physical ones.

# FURTHER READING

The literature on the philosophy of mind is huge. The following represent no more than a limited and personal selection of books that I have found to be particularly helpful.

For a substantial anthology of texts in this area, try *Mind and Cognition*, William Lycan (ed.) (Blackwell Philosophy Anthologies, 2nd edn, 1999).

*The Nature of Mind*, David M. Rosenthal (ed.) (OUP, 1991) is an older anthology, but covers the essential ground for students.

A good summary of the traditional issues, along with a critical assessment of cognitive science, artificial intelligence and functionalism, can be found in John Searle's *The Rediscovery of Mind* (MIT Press, 1992). This book is very clear, hard hitting and readable.

Or try *Philosophy of Mind*, Jaegwon Kim (Westminster Press, 1996).

Also from MIT Press (Massachusetts Institute of Technology) in 1992, there is *The Philosophy of Mind: Classical Problems / Contemporary Issues*, B. Beakey and P. Ludlow (eds), an anthology of readings from Ancient Greece to the present day, giving a fine historical overview of the subject.

On Ancient Greek ideas of the mind and self, see *Companion to Ancient Thought 2: Psychology*, Stephen Emerson (ed.) (CUP, 1991), for a scholarly and thorough outline of this period.

On artificial intelligence, and for a review of the development of cognitive science, see *Minds, Brains and Computers*, R. Cummins and D.D. Cummins (eds) (Blackwell, 2000).

For an easy but sound introduction to consciousness, try *Introducing Consciousness*, Papineau and Selina (Icon, 2000).

David Chalmers' *The Conscious Mind* (OUP, 1996) is an important contribution from an influential philosopher in this area. Not exactly an easy read, but presents a clearly argued alternative to a reductionist approach.

For minds in other species, and the role of language in the development of the human mind, see *Kinds of Minds*, Daniel Dennett (Wiedenfeld & Nicholson, 1996). His other books include *Darwin's Dangerous Idea* and *Consciousness Explained*.

# INDEX